CASE ILLUSTRATION OF PROFESSIONAL ETHICS & PSYCHOTHERAPY CASE STUDIES

CASE ILLUSTRATION OF PROFESSIONAL ETHICS & PSYCHOTHERAPY CASE STUDIES

DR. KALA THOMPSON-TAYLOR

ARPress
ILLUMINATING IDEAS
EMPOWERING VOICES

ARPress
45 Dan Road Suite 5
Canton MA 02021

Hotline: 1(888) 821-0229
Fax: 1(508) 545-7580

Ordering Information:
Quantity sales. Special discounts are available on quantity purchases by corporations, associations, and others. For details, contact the publisher at the address above.

Printed in the United States of America.

ISBN-13:	Paperback	979-8-89330-827-3
	eBook	979-8-89330-829-7
	Hardcover	979-8-89330-828-0

Library of Congress Control Number: 2024901834

Table of Contents

The American Psychological association has identified five general principles, which should govern professional behavior. These principles are in the area of:

Principle A: Beneficence and Nonmaleficence
Principle B: Fidelity and Responsibility
Principle C: Integrity
Principle D: Justice
Principle E. Respect for Peoples Rights and Dignity

Develop a case study in the area of each principle listed above that illustrates a potential breach of professional ethics for each case study, identify and describe the criteria, which would be used to determine whether or not a breach of ethics exist. Describe the behavior that, determine the breach of ethics in your case study. In each case, assume that you are a professional who observes the problem. Describe what action you as a professional psychologist, are required to take. Describe the actions that the offending professional should take to correct the problem.

Principle A: Beneficence and Nonmaleficence

The over-arching goal of psychologist concerning beneficence and nonmaleficence, is to strive to benefit clients who seek treatment, and for psychologist to take care of the client and do no harm to the clients. Further it is the necessity of the psychologist to safeguard and protect the rights of clients and for psychologist to interact with clients in a professional manner. Psychologist, are expected to be conscious of (his or her own mental state of mind to ensure the ability to provide effective treatment to others.

"When conflicts occur among psychologist, they attempt to resolve these conflicts in a responsible fashion to avoid and minimize harm, because psychologist scientific and professional judgments and actions may affect the lives of others, they are to alert and guard against personal, financial, social, organizational, or political factors that might lead to misuse of their influence. Psychologists strive to be aware of the possible effect of their own physical and mental health and their ability to help those with whom they work." (American Psychological Association [APA], Research Code of Conduct 2002).

Case illustration

Dr. John Doe a medical doctor and psychologist has been asked to conduct an assessment and evaluation on a youth after the youth was reported to welfare services by the school nurse after suffering from convulsions because of low iron deficiency. The youth showed signs of poor nutrition and seemed to suffer from depression. The mother did not take the youth to the hospital for proper treatment due to her holistic medical and mental healing beliefs, although the mother was not in favor of traditional medical treatment based on her cultural beliefs she is not opposed to the ideal, either. The school psychiatric nurse believed the youth was simply neglected and reported the incident to welfare authorities.

Based on the mothers religious background and cultural beliefs it may be a dilemma for Dr. John Doe to explain to the welfare authorities regarding why the youth is male nourished and believed to be suffering from depression based on the holistic cultural beliefs of the mother, although the medical and mental health care requirement for children in the hospital setting is not consistent with her cultural beliefs.

Dr. John Doe has several circumstances that may prevent him from being able to provide an effective assessment and health evaluation mainly due to the mother's cultural beliefs. Dr. John Doe must take extraordinary measures to become competent in the understanding of the mothers cultural beliefs to conduct an effective assessment, and health evaluation.

Moreover, as a result Dr. John Doe is not confident of competence because he is not versed in nontraditional healing practices, and realizes that the sensitivity of the time factors in determining the need to produce an effective and accurate assessment and evaluation decision to report to the welfare case workers. Without an accurate understanding of the mothers cultural beliefs, the assessment and evaluation decision by Dr. John Doe may not be a true quantitative analysis of the mother holistic medical beliefs.

Breach of ethics dilemma

Dr. John Doe is required by Standard 2.01(b), to have knowledge of diversity that's effective for implementation of services rendered, seek consultation, or attain supervision to ensure the competence of services and initiate a referral to the appropriate Medical Doctor with psychiatric experience in the field; exception to the rule is emergency services (Standard 2.02). (APA, 2002).

However, in the absence of emergency services Dr. John Doe is in a compromising situation under the current circumstances by not possessing the appropriate knowledge, consultation, supervision, and referral source for the youth's parents.

Action as a professional required to take

If Dr. John Doe does not conduct and assessment and health evaluation or conducts an unreliable assessment or health evaluation that would portray the youth's parents as being neglectful and will result in the youth being placed in foster care and possible criminal proceeding against the parents.

Dr. John Doe knows that he may be in violation of Standard 2.01, which is the importance of the General Principle A: Beneficence and Nonmaleficence in which it is the psychologists' duty according to the American Psychological Association, (2002), "Safeguard the welfare rights of those with whom they interact professionally."

Therefore, Dr. John Doe has a duty in taking the youth's case, and to conduct the assessment and health evaluation objectively while also respecting the client's privacy rights, and confidentiality.

Actions the offending professional should take to correct the problem

In trying to determine how to move forward, Dr. John Doe can consider the following various factors:

1. Acquire supervision or consultation in an efficient manner
2. Seek assistance from other colleagues, hospital staff and, welfare services that can assist with finding a professional experience in the youths family cultural holistic healing back ground.
3. Further educate him-self on the understanding of the parent's holistic healing perspective that would aid in understanding of conducting the assessment and health evaluation that would support the decision made by youth welfare authorities.

4. Risk of conducting an unreliable assessment and health evaluation (to the youth, if the parent is depicted more favorably than the parent is portrayed as more neglectful than is the case) verse the certainty of parent separation from the youth and legal action against the parent if no assessment and evaluation is conducted. In other words out way the benefits of conducting the assessment and health evaluation verse legal action proceeding without it.

Dr. John Doe will have to take a broader comprehensive review to gather information to make an accurate determination.

In this case that is unique is exemplary of the "Breadth of assessment variables and the importance of psychologist adopting unconventional measures to achieve the most valid and accurate results." (Campbell, 2010, p.).

The overarching goal is to ensure the well being and safe guard of the client being served. Therefore, a decision must be made to determine if the benefits out-weigh the legal ramifications on the parent and of the child, and the child not getting adequate treatment to cure his or her health concerns and mental health issue.

Not all decision are "cut and dry" emergency situations arise were medical professional must make a determination when there is very little time to seek the professional advice needed when a health care professional is not well-equipped or experienced enough in the field to make an immediate accurate professional determination. With this grey area lies in determining the professional code of APA conduct, "All" measures of trying to attain the necessary professional assistance needed by the health care professional before making a decision to out-weigh the benefits.

Finally Dr. John Doe should arrange for assistance of the hospitals resource services center to find suitable holistic healers to interview and explain to welfare protective services his concerns of securing adequate informed consent from the parent. In addition to arranging a conference call with the holistic healer and the parent to get a better understanding of the parents actions in relations to the youths deteriorating health problem and depression.

After getting an understanding of the holistic healing process, and the cultural beliefs of the parent and youth family cultural beliefs, it will help Dr. John Doe to understand better traditional healing rituals, and further identify that the parents actions was not a threat to the youth, the parent took the youth to the hospital as an alternative outside the holistic healing because it was not working.

Whereby, establishing a unified census for both sides to work together in deciding the proper medical treatment of the youth. With Dr. John Doe treating the youth with the appropriate medication to deal with the depression, and the appropriate medication to deal with the anemia, although still concurring with the holistic healing process of the parent's beliefs.

In the future medical knowledge is imminent in learning the holistic process among various cultures in society and in order for the medical professional to understand this process; knowledge and understanding is essential to provide and effective assessment, and health evaluation based on having adequate knowledge and understanding of holistic views and rituals.

"Nonmaleficence and beneficence are often viewed as paired principles because they seem to be linked together. Actually, nonmaleficence requires only that you prevent individuals from being harmed. This act of prevention can involve creating an environment where treatment can be practical in a safe manner and where patients can be free from harassment in its many forms. Beneficence requires that you go beyond prevention to ethical action. You work to respect the individualism (I you relationship) of all patients and find ways to nurture them." (Nonmaleficence and Beneficence, Chpt. 3, para. 21).

Moreover, "If you attempt to carry out a task in a given environment, you must be sure that your actions have positive impact in the context. These theories discourage selfish behavior which may directly or indirectly harm or deprive a recipient community. Notions of harm and benefit are molded by context, and thus medical practice, cultural, economic, social religions, political and other factors tie into how nonmaleficence and beneficence are used in ethical decision-making." (The Eisel Project, 2011, para. 3).

Diagnosis and therapy from a holistic perspective

According to Dr. Pelletier, (1987), "Illness is the result of a complex interaction of social factors, physical and, psychological stress, personality, and the inability of the person to adapt adequately to pressures." With this broad view of perspective presents evidence for most of today's major mental health problems.

In holistic medicine according to Dr. Pelletier, (1987), "Psychosomatic is defined as the fundamental interaction between mind and body which is involved in all diseases and all process affecting health maintenance, and in the case illustration of the youths family they believe heavily on this psychosomatic fundamental although the parents sought traditional medicine help out side of their primary holistic beliefs since it was not working.

According to Dr. Sheally, (1993), she emphasizes that "Good nutrition and exercise programs appropriate for each patient." In the case illustration the youth was suffering from inadequate nutrition. "There is also a problem from the standpoint of health care delivery. The holistic approach is time consuming it requires going beyond the physical examination and related diagnostic studies to study the "*Whole Patient*" and the life context that the client lives."

Further, in the context of "Beneficence and Nonmaleficence" according to Milliken, BSN., MSN EdD, (2004), "A legitimate healthcare provider do not make false promises. A legitimate health care provider employs appropriate therapies and encourages each patient, even in the presence of serious illness."

Mental health care professional must be mindful of the decisions made and ethical dilemma that follows the decision made, and to ensure that the treatment services rendered are and always will be in the best interest of the client.

References

1. APA Code of Conduct. (2002). Ethical Principles of psychology and Code of Conduct, including amendments. Retrieved from http://www.apaorg/print-this.aspx

2. APA Research Code of Conduct. (2002. Retrieved from http://www.socsci.uci.edu/APARearchcodeofconduct.pdf.

3. Linda Campbell, Melba Vasquez, Stephen Behnke, Robert Kinchertt, (2010). APA Ethics Case Commentary and Case illustrations.

4. Mary Elizabeth Millken, B.S.N., M.S., EdD., (2004). Understanding Human Behavior

5. Nonmaleficence and Beneficence Chpt. 3. Retrieved from http://samples.jbpub.com/9780763773274/Chapter3.pdf

6. Pelletier, Kenneth R. (1987). Mind as Healer, Mind as Slayer: A Holistic approach to parenting and health and stress disorders.

7. Sheally, C. Norman, & Myss, Caroline M. (1993). The Creation of Health: The Emotional, Psychological, and Spiritual Responses that promote Health and Healing. Walpole NH: Still Point.

8. The Eisel Project, (2011). Beneficence and Non-Maleficence, Para 3. Retrieved from http://ethicsofisl.ubc.ca/?page_id=172

Principle B: Fidelity and Responsibility

Dr. Doe works with at risk youths who have a history of behavioral problems. The problems can range from anger issues, aggressive violent behaviors, to school truancy and, behavioral problems. This family's teenage son is in high school and needs counseling therapy because of his continued truancy and violent school behavioral problems the teenager parents' sought the help of Dr. Doe to help deal with their son behavioral problem. The family is tired of the struggles in dealing with their son and his continued acting out at school and, this is the reason for the referral from the school to Dr. Doe.

The son is very aggressive acting and cruel toward his family by acting out. The family is concerned about the distance it is causing between them and their relationship with him. The family felts that there may be a problem at school that may be causing the outburst, and the aggressive behavior with their son.

The family wants Dr. Doe to discover the problem is causing their sons behavior problems and the acting out at school. The family signed an informed consent document that requires very restrictive access to the session content only. Dr. Doe mission is to ensure the confidentiality of the youth and the information presented is kept confidential unless the youth's life or the life of another person is at risk or child abuse or neglect is a concern.

The concern with Dr. Doe is that the youth is saying that his friends are selling drugs and that he just hangs out with his friends who sell and distribute drugs, and that he does not partake in the selling or distribution of drugs. However, based on the youths activities and aggressive behavior and violence it is apparent that the youth in fact, is involved with the distribution of using of drugs based on some actions, and description of activities that points to his involvement in a variety of disruptive school activities.

Dr. Doe felt the need to meet with the youth's family and ask some additional questions to see if they have any knowledge of their son's actions. The family apparently does not have any additional information to share and was hoping that Dr. Doe can shed some light.

Breach of ethics dilemma

Dr. Doe is highly concerned in "regards" to the confidentiality agreement he made with the youths family and his therapeutic role in working with the youth. Standard 4.02(a) "Allows for psychologist to discuss limited information with clients and patients and in the case with minors, with legal representatives." (APA, 2002). Standard 4.02 (a) also states "The foreseeable use of the information generated through psychological activities."(APA, 2002).

In this case, Dr. Doe have reservations in determining "whether" the activities that the youth is engaging in should outweigh the importance of maintaining confidentiality, which is similar to standard 4.02(a), Standard 10.02(a) states that "Psychologist must clarify at the outset their role in the therapeutic relationship and the probable use of the information obtained through services." (APA, 2002).

Further in the medium Dr. Doe should be concerned if "whether" a waiver of confidentiality, albeit justified, would cause harm to the therapeutic relationship between Dr. Doe and the youth that could result in imminent damage.

Dr. Doe is in a very compromising situation, in dealing with the youths family wanting to know wants going on with their son's behavior. Dr. Doe feels he has to make a decision on "whether" it is appropriate and ethical to discuss the youth problems with the family. Dr. Doe realizes the sole responsibility lies with him and his client's therapeutic needs, and Dr. Doe has conveyed to the family about typical often occurring adolescent behaviors.

Dr. Doe has conveyed the appropriate information to the youth's parents, the informed consent could have been constructed to imply that "only" knowledge of activities that pose a high risk to self or others could compromise confidentiality, because the youth are engaging in illegal activities which could result in legal action or jail time in addition to safety issues.

Dr. Doe is very worried about in his role regarding confidentiality which is solely on him and not sharing information with the youth's family. Dr. Doe role in providing therapeutic treatment has expanded beyond his limitation of his practice related to the client patient of psychological services relationship because the youth's activities can result in criminal sanctions that may implicate Dr. Doe.

Actions as a professional required to take

In this case it draws a fine line of outweighing risk factors and information sharing, and ensuring the protection of the clients confidentially and simply able to address the issue without causing harm or risk to the client. Dr. Doe needs to determine how he is going to approach the youth's parents without violating the confidentiality of the youth and their doctor patient relationship.

**Actions of offending professional should
take to correct the problem:**

1. Dr. Doe should meet with the youth and address his concerns of the youth's actions, the buying and, selling of drugs and the possible use of it, and address safety concerns, and risk factors, and the legal consequences that the youth may be unaware of, by re-directing the therapeutic content and processing the meaning of confidentiality with the youth could maintain the therapeutic relationship.
2. Dr. Doe could work with the youth on identifying the reason for his involvement with the other youths and how he can help the youth eradicate him-self from the group and move into a more positive direction.

3. Dr. Doe can work to build a better relationship with the youth and his family to break the barriers of the youth's need of a sense of belonging to some group and work to help the youth focus on family involvement.

4. Dr. Doe would need to meet with the family and be forthcoming and address the imminent legal and safety concerns of their youths actions, in addition to expressing to the family the need for the parents to be more involved in the youths life, and their willingness to understand better the needs of their son, and to incorporate family therapy into the therapeutic session.

Dr. Doe will have to set up a therapy session for the family to try to rebuild family unity among the youth and his parents along with reestablishing trust, so that the parents as previously stated will be more involved in their son's life and activities outside the home. Building a much stronger relationship between parents and son will allow for the youth to be more open about his school activities and make him feel that he can trust and begin to open to his parents about problems that may affect him.

Concerning fidelity and responsibility psychologist are to ensure a well positive and trustworthy relationship is established with clients who they work with or provide therapy services, and that they have thorough knowledge of his or her skilled profession without dilemma. Further, more psychologist are to identify their roles and obligations and be able to own up to errors and accept responsibility for their actions to cause no further harm.

In addition, it is essential that psychologist confer with other colleagues in the field and gain in site and opinion in treatment services and practice methods. Further, to ensure that they are in compliance with professional codes of conduct and to ensure that optimum services are rendered without personal gain or taking advantage of clients.

According to Niolon, (2004), "This principle builds on Principle A. When most people use the word "Fidelity" they think of "Loyalty" this is a good starting point because in our work, there is an implicit agreement that we are there to help, and the standard for that help is high. We uphold professional standards of conduct, and watch our colleagues to ensure their ethical behavior is in compliance, and consult with other colleagues and learn from one another in order to make an educated choice about what is the best course of action to help our client."

In addition according to Niolon, (2004), "Responsibility goes a bit further. When we make decisions, we have to follow through and deal with the consequences. Maybe you thought a certain course of action would require you to take on some responsibility for a three to four month period. Others build their work on yours and count on you, but after four months you realize this is likely to go on for *another* four months. This doesn't mean you have no choice but to continue; rather, it means you consider carefully the nature of the obligations you take on, and work to find ways to meet them."

Therapist work hard and ensure that they work with an interdisciplinary team to ensure a level of optimum continuum quality of care is provided to the client, the team together brainstorm ideas and level of treatment services to be provided to the client who would be of most beneficence.

According to Behnke (2004), Principle B, Fidelity and, Responsibility, states that "Psychologists Ethical Standard 1.05, Reporting Ethical Violations, codifies the values behind this principle by stating that psychologists take appropriate action when they learn of a colleague whom has engaged in behavior that has resulted, or is likely to result, in substantial harm."

As previously stated it, is the therapist responsibility to report in appropriate activities that may result in grave danger or harm to a client or person and to ensure no harm comes to the client.

(APA, 2010). "Standard 1.05 resolves the dilemma by giving priority to confidentiality. Note how, in doing so, the code protects the client's right to self-determination by placing in the client's hands the choice of whether and how to respond to the ethics violation. The code also protects the psychologist-client relationship by not exposing the treatment to an unwanted breach in its boundary. Balancing these considerations against the important goal of protecting the public, the code promotes the integrity of the treatment relationship and thereby enhances the ability of the psychologist to meet the individual client's clinical needs."

The rule of the American Psychological Association is clearly defined in "regards" to protecting patients right's, although at times there may be some shaded grey areas not so "Cut and Dry." However, it is the ultimate decision for the psychologist to make a sound judgment and assess the situation and determine if the risk factors out weight the beneficence in determining what is ultimately in the best interest of the client.

Moreover, according to the American Psychological Association, (2010), "It is the overarching goal of psychologist to build trust worthy relationships with their clients." Psychologist uphold professional standards of conduct, clarify their professional roles and obligations, accept appropriate responsibility for his or her behavior, and seek to manage conflicts of interest that could lead to exploitation or harm.

References

1. APA Ethics Code 10.02 (a), (2010). Ethical Principles of Psychology and Code of Conduct.
2. APA Ethics Code 4.02(a), (2010). Ethical principles of Psychology and Code of Conduct.
3. American Psychological Association, (2010). Ethical Principles of psychology, and Code of Conduct.
4. Dr. Stephen Behnke APA Ethics Director, (2004). APA New Ethics Code, its value and excellence in Psychological Services. Vol, 35. No. 7. Print version: pg. 88.
5. Richard Niolon, (2004). Ethics: An Introduction Retrieved from http://www.psychpage.com

Principle C: Integrity

Dr. J provides services to families and children and understands the difficulties with working with families and balancing ethical practices with confidentiality, informed consent and, mandated reporting in "regards" to parents with minors. Dr. J. shares this information with the family and explains to the minors as well. Parents have legal rights to sessions that involve a minor Dr. J. request privacy for minors despite the parents possessing legal rights in regard to their child session information.

Dr. J. explains confidentiality to the family and how important it is, further he explained the boundaries of confidentiality and presented a format of examples of harm to self and others and reiterated family expectations in regard to what is expected of them in relations to sharing confidential information among them as a family and separately.

Dr. J. starts providing therapeutic therapy session to the family because they are "All" having problems that involve the need for therapy the couples have marital problems and the couple's daughters are exhibiting behavioral problems in school, along with isolating themselves from their parent's family and friends. The couple's two daughters are twins and both exhibiting the same type of behavioral problems at school.

The parents contacted Dr. J and expressed the need for therapy for their daughters separately in addition to family therapy, and explained that they needed to understand why their daughters are separating themselves from the couple and, to find out the underlying problems' of why they are exhibiting behavioral problems at school.

The couple is hoping that Dr. J will get to the bottom of the problem among the family members. Dr. J agrees to see the daughters separately outside the family therapy sessions hoping that the daughters will feel comfortable enough to discuss the problems they are having at school.

The counseling Dr, J is conducting with the daughter is going superior until Dr. J meets with the parents during therapy sessions, and they begin to disclose the rumors they have herd through their daughters classmates that the twins are engaging in sexual activities and wants Dr. J. to investigate the allegations.

Dr. J rejects the idea the parents requested of him, and the parents rebel by applying pressure on their daughters to disclose their mischievous ways during the family therapy session. Dr. J believe the therapy session has taken a turn for the worse and feel the therapy session are becoming ineffective because of the parents actions.

Dr. J also feels as though the relationship with the twins have been compromised by a lack of trust they may have encountered because to the parents requesting him to probe into the twin's sexual lives and reveal the confidentiality he agreed to maintain separately with the twins.

Dr. J reminded the parents of the confidentiality agreement and the informed consent form they sign authorizing limited confidentiality to the twins.

The parents feel it is not valid given the new discovery of information received. Based on the parent's aggressiveness to pressure Dr. J the twins are losing utmost confidence in Dr. J feeling as though he may collapse to their parents demanding ways. The twins are reluctant to continue their therapy session with Dr. J thinking he is no longer trust worthy and that he may share their confidential information with the parents.

Breach of ethics dilemma

Dr. J has the challenge of reviewing several ethics standards in relations to the informed consent situation. Standard (10.01), describes the elements of informed consent (APA 2010). These are the modalities that Dr. J should consider when faced with having information on how to inform clients and about the nature of therapy involvement with parents and the nature of confidentiality.

Dr. J had discussed previously these codes with the family during the agreement process. Dr. J also disclosed to the parents the limits of confidentiality and certain specific information agreed upon. (APA, 2010). "Standard 10.02(a), required "Psychologist to clarify which individuals are clients, the psychologist relationship with each person, the role of the psychologist and use of the information obtained."

"A parallel to standard 10.02(a) exist in standard 3.07 (Third party request for services), which also applies in this situation because the parents are third parties who requested services for their daughters and according to the Standard "Psychologist must clarify their roles identify the clients and patients, and explain the use of information obtained." (Campbell, Vasquez, Behnke, Kinscherff, 2010, p)

Dr. J feels that he may have an ethical dilemma between parents and daughters regarding the request for information. According to Pomerantz, (2008), "Among the ethical issues especially relevant to group therapy confidentiality is perhaps most concerning." The focus is not on the group therapist maintaining client's confidentiality because this is insured by professional ethics and standards. Instead, "The focus is on the possibility that fellow group members might violate a client's confidentiality." (Barbender, 2002; Barbender et al., 2004; Shaffer & Galinsky, 1989).

Although parents have rights it is essential that Dr. J maintains confidentiality in regards to the twin's rights in order to maintain a healthy therapeutic relationship with the twins and to avoid harm.

At the outset "Group therapies often require clients agreements in writing to hold material in group session confidential, but if clients violate them, such contractual agreements are virtually impossible to enforce." (Shaffer & Galensky, 1989).

Although an agreement may be hard to enforce in this given situation, therapist still have an ethical requirement to uphold the American Psychological Association Codes of Ethics in Responsibility and Fidelity. If the therapist feels the group session are damaging to the client, there is an ethical decision that has to be made in regards to what is in the best interest for all parties involved.

Actions a professional is required to take.

Dr. J needs to ensure he understands the elements of the Standard code of conduct. Dr. J must delineate the complexity of the situation he is in by:

1. Making a decision on the information that was attained and agreed upon
2. Understanding the dynamics of the relationship already established and the paradigm of the relationship with the twins individually already established and the paradigm shift of the relationship he has established with the family.
3. Dr. J must establish what standards apply to the situation and understand how to proceed ethically while maintaining the dynamic relationship among family and individually.
4. Dr. J relationship in accordance with (APA 2010,) standard 10.02a [2]), and his position and the information obtained are becoming confusing and it is essential that Dr. J clarify the modalities of the Standards.

Actions the offending professional should take to correct the problem

Dr. J has several options in resolving this issue for instance:

1. Dr. J can rebuild or continue the therapy sessions to build trust backup with the family
2. Dr. J can work with each patient individually
3. Dr. J can discuss the role of each of each client and the limits of confidentiality again.

4. Dr. J can re-analyze his role as a therapist for the family and the daughters concerning whether he can even effectively carry out his therapy session without it being conflicting.

5. Dr. J must assess his clients concerns about the parents trying of obtain information in regards to the daughters and wanting to cancel the confidentiality agreement and whether his continued services would be beneficial being that this may cause a set-back to services to the daughters if they do not trust his ability to retain confidential information.

6. Dr. J must determine whether the information he retains would be highly significant to the outcomes of the services and whether the parents would be accepting of the terms of the confidential agreement.

Integrity plays an important role in the professional field clients must be able to respect and trust their therapist, and therapist must insure that their integrity is not at risk of being violated or frowned upon based on inappropriate therapy services being rendered that may cause conflict or set backs to clients when third parties are involved in the process.

Psychologist must use caution when working under such conditions to ensure the safe guard of confidentiality and respect of youths rights based on what's agreed upon.

According to Niolon, (2004), "This builds on Principle B, to behaving with integrity means being honest, and keeping your word when you promise something but more than this, it means taking the extra step to make very sure things are clear, offering services of the highest quality, and retaining responsibility for the outcomes of our work. That's why we say that when the answer to an ethical dilemma begins with, "Well, *technically…*" the answer isn't a good one.

This exemplifies the standard of universal moral ethics being applied. Therapist must always be on guard to avoid pitfalls that may be of grave concern to their clients. It is part of our responsibility to go the extra step to make sure our clients understand what they are getting involved in, rather than relying on "the letter of the Ethics code." We may even turn down some work or opportunities because it would not be helpful, or could exploit others."

Integrity to stand up and do the right thing reminds me of this quote, "Have the courage to say no. Have the courage to face the truth. Do the right thing because it is right. These are the magic keys to living your life with integrity." (W. Clemet Stone).

"Our character, however, is shaped by familial and educational teachings, and the guidance of spiritual mentors. Philosophical, cultural and historical influences also shape our integrity, whether we recognize this or not. Daily, we must choose whether to accept or reject these powerful influences for good, or choose a path that will ultimately corrupt our best intentions."(Barbara Killinger, Ph.D, 2011).

The founding principles of the Psychology code of conduct was founded to establish a sense of pride and dignity and self-worth when working as a professional in the field of mental health or any other field for that matter requiring trust of the community among various cultures. Integrity sets the bench mark for building trusting therapeutic relationships with clients.

Therefore, it should never be the intent of a therapist to allow poor judgment, or bad character, or intentional harm to fog their minds in such a way the takes away from positive character.

According to the "*British Psychological Society, (2009),* "Ethical statement of values are, Psychologists value honesty, accuracy, clarity, and fairness in their interactions with all persons, and seek to promote integrity in all facets of their scientific and professional endeavors. standard of honesty and accuracy *Psychologists should:*

(A) Be honest and accurate in representing their professional affiliations and qualifications, including such matters as knowledge, skill, training, education, and experience.
(B) Take reasonable steps to ensure that their qualifications and competences are not misrepresented by others, and to correct any misrepresentations identified.

(C) Be honest and accurate in conveying professional conclusions, opinions, and research findings, and in acknowledging the potential limitations.

(D) Be honest and accurate in representing the financial and other parameters and obligations of supervisory, training, employment, and other contractual relationships.

(E) Ensure that clients are aware from the first contact of costs and methods of payment for the provision of professional services.

(F) Claim only appropriate ownership or credit for their research, published writings, or other scientific and professional contributions, and provide due acknowledgement of the contributions of others to a collaborative work.

(G) Be honest and accurate in advertising their professional services and products, in order to avoid encouraging unrealistic expectations or otherwise misleading the public." The principles of integrity are set in stone across nations in the mental health field every scholar seeks to achieve the same outcomes "*integrity.*"

All of the above modalities are universal beliefs among psychology scholars who study human behavior and the application of the practice. Psychologist must adhere to such universal practices to maintain a standard of excellence.

References

1. APA Code of Conduct (10.01). Ethical Principles of psychologist and Code of Conduct.
2. Andre M. Pomerantz, (2008). Clinical Psychology Science, Practice, and Culture.
3. APA Code of Conduct (10.02(a) & 10.02a[2]. Ethical Principles of Psychology and Code of Conduct.
4. APA Code of Conduct (3.07). Ethical Principles of Psychology and Code of Conduct.
5. Brabender, (2002); Brabender et al., (2004); Shaffer & Galinsky, (1989). Clinical Psychology: Science, Practice, Culture.
6. Barabara Killinger, PhD. (2011). Integrity Doing the Right thing for the Right reason.
7. British Psychological Society, (2009). Code of Ethics and Conduct.
8. Campbell Linda, Vasquez Melba, Behnke Stephen, Kinscherff Robert, (2010). Ethics Code Commentary and case Illustrations.
9. Shaffer & Galensky (1989). Clinical Psychology, Science, Practice, and Culture. (p.266).
10. Niolon (2004). Ethics Introduction. Resources for students and professionals Website: http://www.psychpage.com
11. William. Clement Stone, (2009). The success system that fails.

Principle D: Justice

(APA, 2010), standard case 9.01(C) "When Psychologist, conduct a record review or provide consultation or supervision an individual examination is not warranted or necessary for the opinion, psychologist explain this and the sources of information on which they based their conclusions and recommendations."

Case Illustration

Dr. A receives a call from a colleague who works in the public school system, the colleague is calling in regards to a youth at the high school he works at and is a student in his English class.

The youth is a Mexican kid name Jimmy who is having an adjustment disorder in getting acclimated into the school system, he recently moved from Mexico to California. The evidence suggest that he is an attention seeker and will not stay seated in his chair, causing attraction with fellow class mates, and overall acting out behavioral problems.

The colleague recruited Dr. A because of his skills in psychotherapy and working with troubled youths, and his ability to treat behavioral problems. Dr. A will conduct a battery of test such as, assessments, personality test, and interview the parents as a means to gather as much information on the client's child hood history as possible and into his teen years and environmental structure growing up.

After completing all the necessary evaluations, Dr. A has determined that Jimmy has an (adjustment disorder). Dr. A shares this with Jimmy's parents who are also struggling with the English language and getting acclimated to California as well Dr. A used an interpreter to assist in English translation. Dr. A also shared the evaluation and testing outcomes information with the school system and Jimmy's instructor. Dr. A recommended that Jimmy should be placed in a special class to deal with his problem and establish behavioral intervention. However, unknown to Dr. A Jimmy's math teachers also has noticed some special characteristics and refers him to a psychometrics who has determined that Jimmy is dyslexic and that he reads math problems words out of content.

Breach of ethics Dilemma

Dr. A finds out about this information and he initially feels the diagnosis is another issue out side of his current finding about Jimmy. Dr. A is concerned about the additional findings and is concerned if there are some circumstances surrounding Jimmy's behavior that is making him act out due to the impairment of him being diagnosed with dyslexia.

Dr. A confers with other colleagues about his dilemma and concerns. Dr. A has knowledge that youths generally have behavioral problems and act out when challenged with learning disabilities that may cause embarrassment among peers. It has been observed that children tend to direct attention to themselves when called upon in front of the class by a teacher to answer a question, or to answer a question regarding an assignment in front of the class.

Dr. A feels a little compromised by this new discovery and that his assessment evaluation conducted may be a misdiagnosis based on not identifying educational problems. Dr. A also realizes that he didn't properly follow the intent of: Standard 9.01(a) in that he was not able to evaluate Jimmy's with educational testing materials and does not know how to use the appropriate testing instruments that would have detected Jimmy's reading disorder. Dr. A felt that his expertise in the assessment conducted would suffice.

Actions a professional are required to take

Dr. A realizes he needs to intercept in the remediation and treatment of Jimmy and that he must devise a plan to address Jimmy's diagnosis and establish a better approach to assess Jimmy.

Dr. A will need to learn the assessment trends in the educational system, in addition to taking continuing education classes in the area of educational behavioral problems. Dr. A needs to deliver his feedback to the school and the parents and ensure the youth is assigned to a special education classroom for educational behavioral disorders and to deal with Jimmy's reading disability.

Action offending professional should take to correct problem

There are a few variables that Dr. A can take such as:

1. Dr. A meets with Jimmy's parents and discusses the aspects of his outcomes and treatment recommendations.
2. Further disclose the misrepresentation of his findings based on the error of initial approach.
3. Disclose that his area of expertise in educational behavior problems is limited and unable to give a specific diagnosis for Jimmy's behavioral problem since it may contribute to his dyslexia.

Dr. A further plans to take additional courses in learning disabilities and diversity competence in order to feel confident to conduct an assessment based on educational learning disabilities.

After all of the controversy it is essential that Dr. A meets with the parents of Jimmy and explain to them the issues surrounding his assessment and evaluation and the dilemma of an erroneous assessment being conducted due to lack of knowledge about educational behavioral problems, it will be necessary for Dr. A to describe the nature of his outcomes and the reasons for the error that was made and the approach that lead up to making a mistake in the a prognosis of their sons behavioral problem and how it relates to Jimmy's learning disability, and make recommendations about Jimmy's future moving forward.

However, Dr. A is well aware that a decision in Jimmy's diagnosis cannot be substantiated at this time due to the complexity of Jimmy's disability and the outcomes of his remediation treatment of his learning disability. Jimmy's disability takes first position in determining whether there will be a need for additional services. In addition it is essential that Dr. A further, needs to expand in the area of knowledge in learning disorders in an effort to feel confident in applying this type of services to his practice of therapy services.

Dr. A makes certain that he meets with Jimmy's parents and discloses the discovery of information and the specific implication of the treatment recommendation for Jimmy based on new discovery of a learning disability. Dr. A further gives detail into how he misdiagnosed Jimmy's learning disability and that it may very well be the reason for Jimmy acting out in school.

Dr. A made it clear to the parents that it was human error in his diagnosis of Jimmy's condition and will have to assess the outcomes of his treatment to determine whether in fact Jimmy may need additional therapeutic services in the near future.

Dr. A showed integrity in letting the parents know of his misdiagnosis of Jimmy's condition thereby establishing trust with the parents by acknowledging his error and lack of knowledge in the area of learning disabilities.

According to the American Psychological Association, (2010) "Psychologists recognize that fairness and justice entitle all persons to access to and benefit from the contributions of psychology and to equal quality in the processes, procedures, and services being conducted by psychologists. Psychologists exercise reasonable judgment and take precautions to ensure that their potential biases, the boundaries of their competence, and the limitations of their expertise do not lead to or condone unjust practices.

Moreover, Gillon, (1994), "Emphasis that justice is more than mere equality in that people can be treated unjustly even if they are treated equally. With reference to Aristotle, he argues that it is important to treat equals equally and un-equals unequally in proportion to the morally relevant inequalities (the criterion for which is still being debated).

Situations will always arise where decisions have to be taken and there are limited resources, different options and other conflicting moral concerns. Care must be taken to ensure that health care resources are used sensibly and fairly."

In the everyday practice of therapeutic services, the practice of equality must be balanced to allow fairness of treatment services, and opportunity to all cultural backgrounds in need of services.

"Justice is not listed as an ethical principle because it is less important that the other ethical principles but rather because it involves both the individual relationship between the psychologist and a client or research participant and because psychology is a helping profession and because to some extent the issue of justice can be seen as an extension of beneficence and or trying to do good." (Engel Hardt, 1986; W.D. Ross, 1930). Psychologist need to be concerned with the wider issues of social life.

Moreover, "The formal means of justice have been trace back to "Aristotle, Beauchamp & Childress (1989), "Who argued that justice involved treating individuals equally but in proportion to their relevant differences."

In the case of Dr. A he must decide what is fair principles should never be used as an excuse to treat someone without care or as an object to do so. Noddings, (1984), suggested this "Would diminish the ethical ideal because being ethical depends upon the, "To be Good" and to remain in caring relations to the other."

In the case of Dr. A, he needs to share as previously stated, the new discovery of information with Jimmy's parents that Jimmy's dyslexia may be the underlying cause of Jimmy's behavior despite the inadequate psychological assessment Dr. A conducted and Dr. A's lack of educational knowledge in behavioral problems associated. Aristotle so profoundly stated, "All virtue is summoned upon in dealing justly."

References

1. American Psychological Association, (2010). Ethical Principles of Psychology and Code of Conduct.
2. American psychological Association, (2012). The Ethical Principles of Psychology and Code of Conduct.
3. APA Code of Conduct (9.01) (C), (2010). Ethical Principles of Psychology and Code Of Conduct.
4. APA Code of Conduct 9.01(a), (2010). Ethical Principles of Psychology and Code of Conduct.
5. Aristotle (384BC-322BC). The Quotation Page Website: http://www.quotationpage.com
6. Dr. Raanan Gillon, (1994). Justice: The Four Common bio Ethical principles. Website: http://www.alzeimer-erupe.org
7. Karen Strohm Ketchener, (2000). Foundations of Ethical Practice Research and Teaching in Psychology. (pg.51).

Principle E: Respect for People's Rights and Dignity

Dr. B and Dr. C are in a dilemma about having sexual relations with former clients. Dr. B a psychologist has a practice that focus on evaluations. Most of Dr. B clients are adults and on occasions she may see a few youths when needed due to court orders or the judicial systems requesting such and evaluation. Dr. B provides counseling sessions as a result of the outcomes of the evaluations she conducts. Dr. B attends many networks events and subsequently ran into a previous client she had once provided counseling services to over 6 years ago.

The client reminded Dr. B of the counseling session he used to have with her and the conversation lasted quite a while. During the course of the conversation the pair became attracted to one another and the client asked Dr. B out on a date. Dr. B clearly recalls the client/therapist therapeutic relationship they once had and Dr. B is concerned as to whether the relationship would be in violation of Standard 10.08, "Sexual intimacies with former therapy clients." (APA Code of Conduct, 2010).

Dr. C also ran into a former client at a network event and this client was a former client also from 4 years ago, and had received more than 5 years of therapy treatment from Dr. C she had provided intensive cognitive behavioral therapy treatment to the client over the past 5 years and it was a driven dynamic approach that was very effective for the client, and she cleaned up this clients life. Dr. C kept having run in encounters with the client he had a successful business, and a beautiful home and had never gotten married.

Dr. C. had begun to have an attraction for this client since they continue to have run in's and are always at the same business network events. Although the therapy had ended over 4 years ago well past the 2 year time frame, Dr. C is also concerned about Standard code 10.08, if they begin seeing each other.

Breach of ethnic's dilemma

Both Dr. B and Dr. C are having the same situation with being attracted to former clients, and both Dr. B and Dr. C are concerned about the importance of Standard 10.08, despite the fact that two doctors are interested in rekindling a relationship with former clients. Standard 3.05, "Multiple relationships, remind psychologist, and warns against being in a professional relationship with a client and promising to enter into a relationship in the near future with the same client." (APA, 2002).

This prohibited act also takes the form of Standard 10.08(b) (7) of "Inviting a post therapy intimate relationship." (APA, 2002). Moreover, psychologist put themselves as risk of being exploited when they enter into relationships with previous clients, there are many variable or motives that some clients may have, thereby putting the psychologist in a very compromising situation to be exploited. There have been many news broadcast cases in this instance such as the recent online news broadcast and CNN news broadcast about a psychologist having an affair with a previous client in the jail system. Although she was well pass her 2 year bench mark, she was caught having sex with the inmate while on the job which was a violation of prison policies and a violation of the professional standards code. This psychologist comprised her position by having a relationship with an inmate who later exploited her by being an informant for the prison system resulting in her termination for violation of the American Psychological Association Ethic Codes of Standard and prison rules.

Therefore it is essential that psychologist use extreme caution concerning their intentions of getting into or thinking about getting into a relationship with a client, it falls into the category of *"Buyer*

Beware," in this instance neither Dr. B nor Dr. C are in a current relationship with either past client. Therefore, the 10.08(a), which prohibits sexual intimacies within 2 years, is not in question in this situation. Both of the psychologists have to examine the risk of meeting the Standard 10.08(b).

Standard 1.05 creates an exception when "an intervention would violate confidentiality rights." As an example, this exception may arise when a client relates a sexual involvement with a previous psychologist; the treating psychologist is then faced with an ethical dilemma that requires choosing between the principle of fidelity and responsibility, on one hand, and confidentiality, on the other.

Actions as a professional required to take

Dr. C must consider her actions as a result of getting into a relationship with a previous client under Standard 10.08(b), and her position of providing professional services to the client and the potential harm to the client and the significant implication of the role of psychologist client relationship.

In the case of Dr. C she needs to take into consideration that there may be a possibility of negative impact on the client and regress the condition of therapy the client received, being that it was intense therapy the client received based on a past history of rejection, anger, and betrayal conflict it would possibly exacerbate any post traumatic event and cause harm, which would still be a major factor in the context of the relationship. Therefore, it would not be appropriate to jeopardize the mutual understanding of the therapeutic relationship.

Action the professional should take to correct the problem

1. Both of the psychologist actions reflect on Standard 10.08, and are well aware of the grey areas that surround Standard 10.08 and the stigma that follows and their actions should be to ensure no harm to the client and to safeguard the welfare and rights of clients they provide therapeutic services to: (A: beneficence and

Nonmaleficence), and the right to self-determination and autonomy, (General principle E. Respect for people rights and dignity). Both Dr. B and Dr. C understand that they must make the decision to refrain from getting involved in a relationship with their former clients..

2. Dr. B and Dr. C should be able to demonstrate there was no exploitation or improper acts committed under Standard 10.08(b).

3. Dr. B and Dr. C should repress any feeling they may have toward the client and understand that the relationship cannot be free from characteristics of psychotherapy relationship, and therefore understand that a relationship in a post-therapy situation cannot happen.

According to Campbell, Vasquez, Behnkwe, and Kinscheref, (2010), "Psychologist cannot rely on the testimony of the former clients; instead they should use professional judgment in evaluating the conditions of 10.08(b), seek consultation, and make a reasoned decision on the basis of what they know to be the circumstances of the therapeutic variables, the nature of the therapeutic relationship and their ability to meet the conditions of Standard 10.08(b)."

Further according to Pomerantz, (2008), "One of the characteristics most closely associated with the ethical practice of clinical Psychology is confidentiality. In fact, confidentiality is specifically mentioned among the General Principles (in Principle E: Respect for People's Rights and Dignity) and in numerous specific Ethical Standards, including Standard 4.01, "Maintaining Confidentiality," which begins, "Psychologists have a primary obligation and take reasonable to confidential information..." (American Psychological Association, 2002, p. 1066). There is good reason for the emphasis on confidentiality in the profession of psychology: Our profession is entrusted by the public to provide professional services without sharing the private, personal details offered in the process."

Therefore respect for client's rights and dignity falls in alignment with the guiding principals' of the American Psychological Association professional ethics of standard and principles. Although Dr. B and Dr.

C had opportunities to engage themselves in a perfectly acceptable relationship with former clients and were well pass the two year "Bench Mark" of engaging in sexual intimacy with former clients. The Doctors had to make a wise decision and think about the variables of professional ethics that may cause harm despite the two year waiting period. As a rule of thumb many scholars have implied *"Never"* risk professional ethics at any time and maintain optimum standards of practice.

References

1. APA Code of Conduct (3.05), (2010). Ethical Principles of psychology and Code of Conduct.
2. APA Code of Conduct (10.08), (2010). Ethical Principles of psychology and Code of Conduct.
3. APA Code of Conduct (10.08) (a), (2010). Ethical Principles of psychology and Code of Conduct.
4. APA Code of Conduct ((10.08) (b) (7), (2010). Ethical Principles of psychology and Code of Conduct.
5. American Psychological Association, (2002). (2010). Ethical Principles of psychology and Code of Conduct.
6. American Psychological Association Code of Ethics Chapter 5. (p.84)
7. Andre M. Pomerantz, (2008). Clinical psychology Science, Practice, and Culture.
8. Linda Campbell, MelbaVasquez, Stephen Behnkwe, and Robert Kinscheref, (2010). APA, Ethics Code Commentary and case Illustration.

Discuss the role of psychological assessment in counseling or clinical practice. What are the strengths and weaknesses inherent in formal psychological testing? Why might you choose formal psychological testing techniques and for what types of clients? What limitations should be considered: Are there different considerations for objective and subjective assessment techniques?

Assessment

The assessment process is the beginning of identifying and understanding human behavior and building a relationship with a client by obtaining history information on a client and gathering enough information to establish a mental disorder according to the DSMV IV criteria of diagnosis of mental illness in a patient.

Role of psychological assessment in clinical practice

The role of psychological assessment in counseling and clinical practices is a way to asses an individual's ability to carry out daily living activities. "According to Michel Hersen, Ph.D" There is a rich historical emphasis on scientific inquiry through careful assessment and observation in the field of clinical psychology as evidenced by such popular training models as the scientist-practitioner model (Benjamin & Baker, 2000) and local clinical scientist model (Stricker & Trierweiler,1995)."

In these modalities psychologist integrated the concept of theory and research in the assessment process, diagnosis and treatment planning. Based on many psychological readings it is understood that scientific research suggest psychologist should have of the means of measuring systematically how they proceed with their session and if their clients are making positive outcomes.

Strengths and weaknesses inherent in psychological testing?

The strengths of assessment are improved quality of care, research possibilities, identifying mental health or substance abuse problems. On the contrary some of the weakness in assessments are lack of interest, over whelming paper work for the clients, lack of agreement,

Why choose formal psychological testing techniques

Limitations to be considered

Considerations for objective and subjective techniques.

On the contrary when it comes to psychological counseling, 'According to Maloney and Ward (1976), "A psychological assessment is the attempt of a skilled professional, usually a psychologist, to use the techniques and tools of psychology to learn either general or specific facts about another person, either to inform others of how they function now, or to predict their behavior and functioning in the future." Maloney and Ward (1976) offer that assessment:

- Frequently uses tests
- Typically docs not involved defined procedures or steps
- Contributes to some decision process to some problem, often by redefining the problem, breaking the problem down into smaller pieces, or highlighting some part(s) of the problem
- Requires the examiner to consider, evaluate, and integrate the data
- Produces results that cannot be evaluated solely on psychometric grounds
- Is less routine and inflexible, and more individualized.

The point of assessment is often diagnosis or classification. These are the act of placing a person in a strictly or loosely defined category of people. This allows us to quickly understand what they are like in general, and to assess the presence of other relevant characteristics based upon people similar to them." Further according to Maloney and Ward, (1976), "There are several parts to assessment:

The Assessment Interview

Note that an assessment interview can be conducted in many ways and for a variety of purposes. Below are several aspects in which to view an interview.

- Verbal and face-to-face - what does the client tell you? How much information are they willing able to provide?
- Para-verbal- how does the client speak? At normal pace, tone, volume, inflection? What is their command of English, how well do they choose their words? Do they pick up on non-verbal cues for speech and turn taking? How organized is their speech?
- Situation - Is the client cooperative? Is their participation voluntary? For what purpose is the interview conducted? Where is the interview conducted?

There are really two kinds of assessment interviews, structured or unstructured.

- Structured - The SCID-R is the Structured Clinical Interview for the DSM-III-R and is, as the name implies, an example of a very structured. It is designed to provide a diagnosis for a client by detailed questioning of the client in a "yes or no" or "definitely somewhat not at all" forced choice format. It is broken up into different sections reflecting the diagnosis in question. Often Structured interviews use closed questions, which require a simple pre-determined answer. Examples of closed questions are "When did this problem begin? Was there any particular stressor going on at that time? Can you tell me about how this problem started?" Closed interviews are better suited for specific information gathering.

- Unstructured - Other interviews can be less structured and allow the client more control over the topic and direction of the interview. Unstructured interviews are better suited for general information gathering, and structured interviews for specific information gathering. Unstructured interviews often use open questions, which ask for more explanation and elaboration on the part of the client. Examples of open questions are "What was happening in your life when this problem started? How did you feel then? How did this all start?" Open interviews are better suited for general information gathering.

Interviews can be used for clinical purposes (such as the SCID-R) or for research purposes (such as to determine moral development or ego state).

Assessment Testing

Listed are eight types of assessment tests:

- Group educational tests such as the California Achievement Test
- The Myers-Briggs
- LD and neuropsychology tests such as the Halstead Reitan Battery
- Intelligence tests the WAIS and WISC
- The Metropolitan Readiness Tests
- Adolescent Substance Abuse Subtle (SSAI-A2)
- Minnesota Multiphasic Personality Inventory MMPI2 or PAI
- interpreted tests, staff skill level of test

Good Assessment Requires

- Complete assessment with good test scores
- Skilled staff who know proper use of testing
- Thorough understanding of Standard Error of Measurement

- Ensure accurate assessment
- Accurate assessment tools
- Give feedback and support in the assessment process.

Strengths and weakness in psychological testing

"Modern psychology has been co-opted by the disease model. We've become too preoccupied with repairing damage when our focus should be on building strength and resilience, especially in children. (Seligman, 2003). Point and case although, many scholars might refute that assessments have become unbalanced over the last century and have moved in a direction of establishing some sort of medium based on conceptualization of weakness, with the other half of the medium being focused strengths. In general this statement may contrast the "average bias" in psychological evaluations over the last century.

"A large number of Psychologist who are uncertain of "smiley face" reports that are more incline to shift more towards strengths, yet illicit vague positive "statements that aren't very helpful in conceptualizing the case, and may even mislead the therapist into under-estimating the difficulties the person will face in changing and benefiting from services, which ultimately hurts the client." (Psychpage.com, para. 2)

According to Borrowing from B. A. Wright's, (1991), he "Suggests, a balanced approach is advocated for gathering information and writing the subsequent report. Specifically, it is suggested that the clinician attend to four aspects of an interviewee: (a) the strengths in the client's psychological makeup, (b) the weaknesses in the client's psychological makeup, (c) the strengths in the client's environment, and (d) the weaknesses in the client's environment. Additionally, using hope theory C. R. Snyder, (1994) as a framework, "The importance of including information about client goals, along with the routes to those goals (pathways thinking) and the motivation to use those pathways (agency thinking), is described. Furthermore, the implications of using this framework in conducting a diagnostic interview and writing the ensuing report are provided. Finally, the advantages of including human strengths are to achieve a balanced interview and report."

Moreover, "In the new millennium, school psychologists have increasingly recognized alternatives to a deficit-based perspective regarding assessment, practice, and research that emerged from the historical disease model of human functioning pervasive in the field of psychology." (Buckley, Storino, & Saarni,2003; Rhee, Furlong, Turner, & Harari, 2001; Terjesen, Jacofsky, Froh, & DiGiuseppe, 2004).

Assessment testing have become a universal concern across the globe. Many health care organizations, and mental health facilities, educational system and employment agencies use assessment testing to identify with understanding human behavior, knowledge and skill set.

"The recent zeitgeist in the field of psychology includes an emphasis on positive psychology." (Huebner & Gilman, 2003; Seligman & Csikszentmihalyi, 2000; Seligman, Reivich, Jaycox, & Gillham, 1995). In addition, "The perspective that wellness is more than the absence of disease symptoms. Positive psychology advocates a change from a preoccupation with solely repairing the worst things in life to also building the best qualities in life." (Seligman, 2002).

Wellness is a vital key to staying mentally stable and focused in a positive way. Assessment testing helps to delineate from symptoms of disease and illness.

'The building of strengths and an emphasis on the prevention of problems are at the forefront of positive psychology." (Seligman & Peterson, 2000). "Likewise, the emerging emphasis on promoting "developmental assets" has focused on the strengths of youths, families, and communities." (Scales & Leffert, 1999). Scales and Leffert, (1999) describe developmental assets as "The positive relationships, opportunities, competencies, values, and self-perceptions that youth need to succeed." Further, "School psychologists have long endorsed strength-based perspectives." (e.g., Lambert, 1964), and during, "The past decade, there has been a growing recognition and an emphasis to embrace this perspective that is promoted among some school psychology practitioners and researchers." (Baker, Dilly, Aupperlee, & Patil, 2003; Chafouleas & Bray, 2004; Doll & Lyon, 1998; Miller, 1998; Nettles, Mucherah, & Jones, 2000; Rhee et al., 2001; Robertson,

Harding, & Morrison, 1998; Smokowski, Reynolds, & Bezruczko, 1999; Terjesen et al., 2004)."

Further "Strength-based assessment can promote a positive arena for school psychologists, teachers, and families to monitor student performance and communicate with success. The endorsement of strengths can empower children and families to take responsibility and navigate their own life experiences." (Rhee et al., 2001). In addition, "School personnel benefit personally from implementing such an approach through increased optimism, hope, and motivation for change that comes from examining strengths and competencies rather than feeling overwhelmed and hopeless by a focus on multiple problems." (Clark, 1999; Constantine, Benard, & Diaz, 1999).

Examples of strength based assessments:

As psychologists have begun to examine aspects of positive psychology more critically, various instruments have been developed for research and clinical practice. Epstein and Sharma (1998) define strength-based assessment as:

The measurement of those emotional and behavioral skills, competencies, and characteristics that create a sense of personal accomplishment; contribute to satisfying relationships with family members, peers, and adults; enhance one's ability to deal with adversity and stress; and promote one's personal, social, and academic development. (p. 3) a variety of instruments are available to objectively assess variables related to strengths and resiliency among youth. Brief overviews of selected strength-oriented assessments are provided in the following table as an introduction to a sampling of such measures."

Limitations of strength and weakness inherent in psychology testing

According to Jimerson, Sharkey, Nyborg, and Furlong (2004), "Strength-based assessment and intervention practices are based on strength building, rather than deficiency focused and, when included in a multidimensional assessment, allow for a more "balanced" approach to viewing youth development. Moreover, employing this approach to assessment enhances the practice of school-based consultation, collaboration, and intervention.

Despite the intuitive benefits of seeking enriched information about the strengths of children, it is acknowledged that there is little empirical data examining available strength oriented measures (e.g., BERS and CHKS) in promoting positive youth development. Only recently have studies began to more rigorously examine these "strength-based" instruments' ability to reliably assess positive indicators and predict positive youth outcomes." (Scales et al., 2000).

Furthermore, as school psychologists expand their use of strength based assessment resources, it is essential that they base practice on more than ideological preferences; thus, further research is necessary to clarify and delineate the value of assessing strengths and the model, paradigms, or theories that drive their use.

Furthermore, as school psychologists expand their use of strength based assessment resources, it is essential that psychologist base practice on more than ideological preferences. Further research is necessary to clarify and delineate the value of assessing strengths and the model, paradigms, or theories that drive their use.

Though longitudinal studies have examined the relative influences of measured risk and protective factors on targeted developmental outcomes, there is limited research examining the relative merits and limitations of a strength-based approach to assessment in the school context. Further research investigating the value-added of considering strengths, in addition to risk factors is essential. Often the focus of related research has examined the value of predicting problems; however, a strength-based approach suggests that it is desirable to examine positive outcomes as well.

While positive psychology has appealed to many scholars and professionals, there is limited empirical investigation that delineates the merits of this perspective in working with children or families. Further research explicating how strengths can be used to facilitate positive youth development is important to enhance school psychology assessment practices. Evidence is needed that a strength-based assessment considers a balance of student needs and skills that provides more comprehensive and meaningful information than traditional deficit-focused models. Ultimately, strength-based assessments must be more than a set of loosely arranged principles or assessment practices, and organized by models that lead to better understanding of all students.

Why choose formal psychological testing techniques

Formal assessment testing techniques are essential in conducting a thorough assessment on a client this is a vital part of the assessment process when making an accurate assessment of a client's needs. The American School Counseling and Association in Assessment Counseling, of the American Counseling Association, found that "73% of the respondents indicated that test were very important in helping them carry out their work. In addition, psychologist in many different setting uses the same assessment instrument." (Bubenzer, Zimpfer, and Mahrle (1990). "Found that community mental counselors are more likely to use Minnesota Multiphasic Personality Inventory (MMPI), along with a few other instrument assessments testing's listed previously."

The MMPI, is used widely across many states, and a very effective assessment tool that helps psychologist carry out their job more effectively in identifying with clients needs based on the MMPI scores attained.

Additional information on psychological testing techniques

"Some studies have documented that counseling outcomes are enhanced when testing is incorporated into the counseling process." (Sexton, Whiston, Walz, & Bleuer, 1997)." Further, Duckworth (1990), Contends that, "When "good" test are used, the counselor can gain insight into the client more rapidly than relying on counseling alone, and Problems are delineated in an effective manner, treatment can be initiated sooner." Duckworth (1990), "Further suggest that test enrich the counseling in the following ways:

- Assessment testing as an aid to focusing on development
- Assessment testing as an aid to problem solving
- Assessment testing as an aid to decision making
- Assessment testing used in psycho-educational manner

Some of the psychological testing techniques most commonly used according to." Duckworth (1990) are:

1. Minnesota Multiphasic Personality Inventory, The **Minnesota Multiphasic Personality Inventory** (MMPI-2, is one of the most frequently used **personality** tests in mental health for all age group category.
2. Substance Abuse Subtle Screening inventory SASSI-3 which "The **SASSI-3** is designed exclusively as a tool for clinical assessment and treatment designed to use for youths and adults.
3. The **Wechsler** Adult **Intelligence Scale** (WAIS) is a test designed to measure **intelligence** in adults and older adolescents."

Although there is a host of assessment techniques that can be used in the field of counseling the following mental health modalities listed have been by far the most universally widely formal used assessment instrument tools.

What type of clients

Assessment testing is conducted on a wide range of clients who may be in need of psychological services, educational services, or employment services. The educational systems conduct's star-testing, and disability learning testing on students to determine their academic learning abilities. Drug treatment facilities or mental health facilities conduct testing on clients who may be suffering from depression, dual diagnosis, suicidal thoughts, psychosis, or paranoid schizophrenia. The prison systems conducts testing on inmate clients who may be in need of psych medications due to a pre-existing mental health problem, or suffering from adjustment disorder while adapting to prison life.

Assessment testing helps identifying criminal behavioral thoughts in the prison system. Assessment testing can also be used on genesis children with high I-Qs, to measure level of knowledge base. Assessment testing is used in a universal perspective in many ways.

Considerations for objective and subjective assessment techniques

According to Atherton J. S (2011), "All assessment is ultimately subjective: there is no such thing as an "objective test". Even when there is a high degree of standardization, the judgment of what things are tested and what constitutes a criterion of satisfactory performance is in the hands of the assessor. However, we can still make every effort to ensure that assessment is valid, reliable and fair.

According to Whinston (2000), "**Objective & Subjective**," are categorized as methods used to score the assessment tool. Many instruments are scored objectively; that is there are predetermined methods for scoring the assessment and no judgments are required by the individual doing the scoring. Subjective instruments require that the individual make professional judgments in scoring the assessments."

For example, most tests are multiple-choice and are objective instruments, and making notation that the scores to the single response are incorrect or correct. Generally speaking essay testing are subjective instruments since the person who is reviewing the exam must make some sort of judgment about the answers to the examinations and its quality. According to Whinston, (2000), "Objectively scored instruments attempt to control for bias and inconsistencies in scoring. In counseling however, we are often interested in exploring issues in people's lives, which are not easily assessed using only objective methods."

References

1. Atherton J. S. (2011). Teaching and learning: Assessment Website: http://www.learningandteaching/teching/assessment.htm

2. B.A. Wrights (1991). Balancing psychological assessments including strengths and hope in clients reports.

3. Baker, J.A., Dilly, L.J., Aupperlee, J.L., & Pattil, S.A. (2003). The development context of school satisfaction: School as psychological healthy environments. School psychology quarterly, 18, 206-221.

4. Baker, Dilly, Aupperlee, & Patil, (2003); Chafouleas & Bray, (2004); Doll & Lyon, (1998); Nettles, Mucherah, & Jones (2000); Rhee et al (2001); Robertson, Harding & Morrison, (1998); Smokoski Reynods & Bezrucko, (1999); Terjesen et al. (2004).

5. Buckley, M. Storino (2004); Saarni, C. (2003). Promoting emotional competence in children and adolescents: Implications for school psychologist. School Psychology Quarterly, 18, 177-191.

6. Bubenzer, Zimpfer and Mahrle (1990). Principles and Applications Assessment in Counseling.

7. Clark, M.D. (1999). Strength-based practice: The ABC's of working with adolescents who don't want to work with you. Retrieved February 27, 2001, from http://www.drugs.indiana.edu/prevention/assets/asset2.html. Constantine, N., Bernard, B., & Diaz, M. (1999). Measuring protective factors and resilience traits in youth: The Healthy Kids Resilience assessment. Paper presented at the Seventh Annual Meeting of the Society for Prevention Research, New Orleans, LA.

8. C.R. Synder, (1994). The Psychology of Hope. New York: Free Press.

9. Duckworth (1990). Positive Psychology in Clinical Practice. Annual review of Clinical Psychology. Vol. 1: 629-651 (Volume publication date 2005).

10. Huebner E. S., & Gillman, R. (2003). Toward a focus on positive psychology in school psychology. School psychology Quarterly,

19(2), 99-102; Seligman & Csikszentmihalyi, (2000); Seligman, M.E.P., Reivich, K, Jaycox, L., & Gillham, J., (1995). The optimistic child. New York: Houghton Mifflin.

11. Lambert, N. M. (1964). The Protection and Promotion of Mental Health in schools. (Public Health Services Publication, No. 1226. 4003342015). Washington DC: US Dept. of Health, Education, Welfare, Public Health Services, national Institute of Health, National Institute of Mental Health.

12. Leffert, N. Benson, P.L., Scales, P.C. Sharma, A. R. Drake, D.R. & Blyth, D.A. (1998). Development assets: measurement and prediction of risk behaviors among adolescents. Applied Developmental Science, 2(4), 209-230.

13. Maloney and Ward (1976). Psychological Assessment Website: http://highered.mcgraw-hill.com/sites/dl/free/0072887672/128838/PsychologicalTesting_Assessmentt.pdf

14. Rapp, C.A. (1997). Preface. In D. Saleeby (Ed.), the strengths perspective in social work practice. New York: Longman.

15. Rhee, Furlong, Turner, & Harari, (2001). Integrating strength-based perspectives in psycho educational evaluation; Terjesen, Jacofsky, Froh, & DiGiuseppe, (2004). Integrating positive psychology into schools: Implications for practice. Psychology in schools, 41(1), 163-172.

16. Rhee, S., Furlong, M. Turner, J & Harari, I. (2001). Integrating strength-based perspectives in psycho educational evaluation. The California Psychologist, 6, 5-17.

17. Scales, P.C. & Leffert, N. (1999). Developmental assets: A synthesis of the scientific research on adolescent development. Minneapolis, MN: Search Institute.

18. Scales, P.C. Benson, P.L. Leffert, N.., & Blyth, D.A. (2000). Contribution of developmental assets to the prediction of thriving among adolescents. Applied Developmental Science, 4, 27-46.

19. Seligman, M.E.P. (2002). Positive psychology, positive prevention, and positive therapy. In C.R. Snyder & S.J. Lopez (Eds.), Handbook of positive psychology (pp. 3-9). New York: Oxford University press.

20. Seligman, M.E. P. (2003). Quote from APA Positive psychology website. Retrieved December 20, 2003, from http:///www.apa.org/release/positivepsy.html.

21. Seligman, M.E.P., & Peterson, C. (2000). Positive clinical psychology. Retrieved December 20, 2003, from http://psych.upen.edu/seligman/posclinpsychchap.html.

22. Sexton, Whinston, Waltz, & Bleuer, (1997). Integrating outcomes research info Counseling Practice and Training. American Counseling Association: Alexandria. VA.

23. Sharma (1998). A strength based approach working with youth and families.

24. Sharkey, Nyborg, and Furlong (2004). The Santa Barbara and Risk Assessment to predict recidivism among male and female juveniles: An investigation of inter-rater reliability and predictive validity. Education and Treatment of Children, 27(4), pp. 353-373.

25. The Standards for Educational and Psychological Testing. (1985).

26. Susan C. Whinston (2000). Principles and Applications of Assessments in Counseling

Historical, socioeconomic and cultural factors influence our understanding of human behavior. Select the developmental stage theory of your choice. Explain how these factors shaped the current understanding of human behavior in 21 century Western thought. What areas of human development do you perceive to be "constant" (both within and across cultures? What aspects of developmental stage theory are more likely to be determined by cultural factors: What current societal trends and changes do you think will influence the next wave of developmental stage theories?

Developmental Psychology

Understanding human behavior in the 21ˢᵗ century Western thought

According to Matsumoto (1989), "If things continue as they have until now, cross-cultural psychology as we know it today will cease to exist in the 21ˢᵗ century. Instead, it will be integrated into mainstream psychology. Yet that integration should not be a total assimilation of cross-cultural psychology into mainstream psychology.

There will be major accommodations as well, fundamentally changing the essence of the way we model and study human behavior. We are already witness to these changes, as we are in the middle of an evolution in psychology." With time comes change and in today's economy the social environment is definitely moving in to a more cross cultural medium as we examine and discuss the era and direction developmental psychology is moving into.

According to Matsumoto (1989), "In the past, cross-cultural psychology was perceived as an "exotic" branch of psychology for those with esoteric interests in culture. Cross-cultural studies were generally viewed as an interesting aberrant of more serious research in mainstream psychology and were generally not assimilated into mainstream knowledge.

Today, however, cross-cultural psychology is viewed as a serious endeavor. Studies reporting cultural differences are widespread and common and make fundamental challenges to mainstream knowledge. Throughout this history, a common thread ties much of this literature together, and that is its overwhelming concern with uncovering universal and culturally specific aspects of behavior."

I believe this to be true to say the least the understanding of cultural beliefs is essential in the effects and understanding of social changes and globalization. In my observations over the last decade there has been a great astronomical social transformation on a global scale the cultural forces that move society into a cross cultural globalization is advancement in technology such as computers, the internet and cable TV, as more expanded trends in the 21st century are expected to evolve.

On the contrary research according to R Triandis, Leung, Villareal, & Clack, (1985), Recent advances in cross-cultural methods include the development of ways to measure IC tendencies on the individual level. Triandis refers to these tendencies as idiocentrism and allocentrism, and their measurement is a major plus for research. They allow researchers to empirically ascertain that their samples differ on this construct, providing an important methodological check and eliminating reliance on anecdotes, impressions, or stereotype when interpreting findings.

They also allow researchers to assess numerically the degree of within-culture variability on this important construct. Using this index, researchers can determine how much of the difference between the groups are attributable to individual level differences in IC. Say, for example, that a researcher intends to compare two cultures where all participants completed an individual level measurement of IC. Group differences on the dependent variable could be tested through normal procedures (e.g., t-test, ANOVA, chi-square, etc.). In addition, the relationship between IC and the dependent variable could be assessed through correlational procedures.

Therefore, if correlations existed, their influence on the group differences obtained earlier could be tested using multiple regression or analysis of covariance (ANACOVA). The degree of contribution of IC to the group differences could be computed by comparing effect sizes of the group between the original and ANACOVA analyses.

"Recent approaches involve a multi-method approach assessing IC tendencies across attitudes, values, opinions, and beliefs. Singelis, Triandis, Bhawuk, and Gelfand (1995) have also developed measurement procedures to assess horizontal and vertical IC. Hui (1988) developed a context-specific method of measurement, while Yamaguchi (1994) has developed more specific measures of collectivism. We have also developed a measure of IC tendencies in specific contexts based on social interaction (Matsumoto et al., 1997).

Areas of human development "constant" both within and across cultures

"Nations, regions and cultural zones form a three-level hierarchy, with nations nested inside regions and regions inside cultural zones. From this perspective, the question is whether there are 'frictions' in the cross-level translation of the two linkages of human development: 'Do these linkages translate from the national to the regional to the cultural zone level with or without frictions?' If there are frictions, human development could not be considered as a general theory because its linkages would vary depending on the level at which they are observed.

Using regression models, such frictions become evident to the extent that the intercepts and slopes of the two human development linkages vary at different levels of aggregation.

As Table 4 demonstrates, the human development linkages do not substantially vary in either their intercepts or slopes at different levels of aggregation. Whether at the national, regional or cultural zone level, intercepts and slopes remain virtually constant. The correlations, of course, increase systematically with higher levels of aggregation, indicating that random variation among lower-level units is averaged out through aggregation to higher level units. Yet, apart from the correlations, neither intercepts nor slopes vary at different levels of aggregation, showing that human development translates without frictions from lower to higher levels of aggregation. "(European Consortium for Political Research, 2003).

Moving on, each of the gray shadowed areas in Table 3 summarizes a group of nations in a distinguished cultural zone. "The first criterion of this classification is religious tradition, which produces 18 countries with a historically Protestant tradition; 27 Catholic countries; 10

Christian Orthodox countries; 10 Islamic countries; and a residual category of 5 countries in the tradition of an 'Asian' religion, such as Buddhism, Hinduism or Confucianism (a quasi-religion).

These five religious groups were subdivided for region or imperial legacy, if there were enough cases to allow for such a division. Thus, the Catholic countries were divided into the zones of 'Catholic Western Europe', 'Catholic Eastern Europe' and 'Latin America.' The division between Western and Eastern Europe reflects whether a country belonged to the Soviet communist empire or not. Latin America as well not only represents an own region, but is distinguished by its Iberian imperial legacy. "

For some countries, specific decisions had to be made. Among the Asian countries, we saw no criterion to group China and India together with other nations." According to Huntington (1996), both of these countries, each with a population of more than one billion, represents a 'civilization' of its own. On the other hand, Japan, South Korea and Taiwan share a Confucian tradition and have in common that they are economically far advanced. Thus we summarized them as 'Developed Far East' moreover, Estonia and Latvia, although having a Protestant tradition, were grouped with the Catholic Eastern European countries with which they share the legacy of Soviet communism and the tradition of 'Western Christianity', as opposed to Orthodox Eastern Christendom (Huntington 1996: 159).

Finally, "The Sub-Saharan countries have not been divided on the basis of religion. Although there are Christian and Islamic influences in Sub-Saharan Africa, there remain specific Black African imprints, based on this region's animist religious roots and its distinctive ethnic make-up. This justifies classifying the Sub-Saharan countries as a specific cultural zone." (Huntington 1996).

In theory religion has played a vital part in the culture of many countries, this sets the bench-mark for developmental stages of development based on cultural religious beliefs and community upbringing within each individuals own country. Religion is strongly rooted in many cultures and plays a vital role in the developmental process.

Aspects of development to be determined by cultural factors

According to Ratner, (1999), "Most cross-cultural psychology focuses on describing the psychology of different peoples without attempting to explain the cultural basis of these psychological differences.

A typical conclusion is that Liberians recall things in context and have difficulty with "Free Recall" (remembering things individually, out of context), while Americans readily employ free recall. Descriptions of mnemonic strategies, perception, emotions, mental illness, and modes of conflict resolution are fascinating. However, they are uninformative about how psychological phenomena are cultural. They are silent about what culture is and how it generates psychological differences among people. Culture is construed as a platform on which psychology rests which is external to psychology rather than as constituting psychology, i.e., penetrating into psychology"

We may say that this approach to cross-cultural psychology studies psychology in culture rather than culture in psychology. The platform model requires little understanding of culture (in general or in particular) because culture is not brought into contact with psychology."

Further Ratner, (2006), asserts "Although cross-cultural psychology has advanced our understanding of cultural aspects of psychology, it is marred by theoretical and methodological flaws. These flaws include misunderstanding cultural issues and the manner in which they bear on psychology; obscuring the relation between biology, culture, and psychology; inadequately defining and measuring cultural factors and psychological phenomena; erroneously analyzing data and drawing faulty conclusions about the cultural character of psychology."

Moreover, "Certain cross-cultural psychologists seek to identify psychological effects of concrete cultural factors rather than abstract variables. This well-intentioned attempt frequently fails because psychologists are insufficiently informed about sociology and history. Extensive, sophisticated knowledge of these areas is necessary if one is to understand a culture and its effects on psychology.

Yet psychologists receive little training in the social sciences, humanities, or philosophy because psychology has been institutionally segregated from them and ideologically oriented toward intra-individual processes. Thus, psychologists' ignorance is not simply due to the vastness and complexity of cultural information which might escape the most diligent researcher. It is due to an entrenched blindness to crucial social issues. This leads to misconstruing cultural factors and their psychological effects." (Carl Ratner 2003).

This problem is found in Peng's cultural analysis of inferential reasoning (Peng & Nisbett, 1999; Peng, Ames, & Knowles, 2001; Ji, Peng, & Nisbett, 2000; Nisbett, Peng, Choi, & Norenzayan, 2001). "The analysis traces psychological differences in oriental and Western reasoning to historical differences in social practices and values of Chinese and Greeks." (Nisbett, et al. 2001, pp. 293-295, 303). Briefly summarized, Peng and his colleagues argue that in ancient times, in the orient:

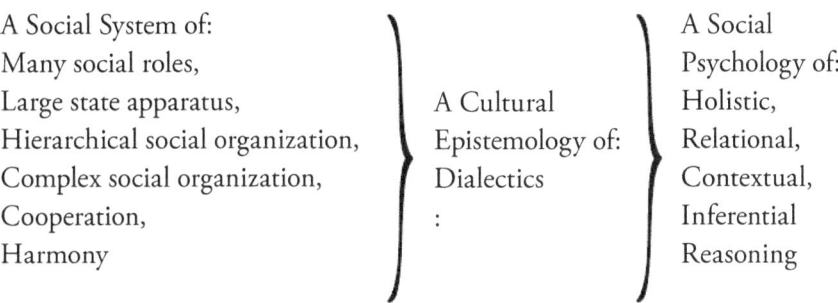

| A Social System of:
Many social roles,
Large state apparatus,
Hierarchical social organization,
Complex social organization,
Cooperation,
Harmony | A Cultural
Epistemology of:
Dialectics
: | A Social
Psychology of:
Holistic,
Relational,
Contextual,
Inferential
Reasoning |

In Ancient Greece: Table 3

| A Social Structure of:
Few social roles
Simple organization
Hunting, fishing,
herding, trading
Decentralized,
individualized
organization
Conflict | A Cultural
Epistemology of:

Formal logic | A Psychology of:
Analytical,
Fragmented,
Linear
Inferential reasoning |

The authors contend that this model persists today: "There is substantial evidence that the social psychological differences characteristic of ancient China and Greece do in fact persist" (ibid., p. 295). Therefore, contemporary Western fragmented, linear reasoning is rooted in the very birth of Western civilization, extending back to philosophy and social conditions thousands of years ago. Contemporary holistic oriental reasoning is similarly rooted in philosophy and social conditions thousands of years old.

Societal trends and changes that will influence next wave of development state theories.

As many would say human development is a cultural magnet and that humans are biological species and are categorized based on our culture involvement.

Many of us are in tune with both our culture and biological heritage to use our language and other cultural tools to learn from each other. "Scholars have recognized that understanding cultural aspects of human development are important for resolving pressing practical problems as well as for progress in understanding the nature of human development in worldwide terms. Cultural research is necessary to move beyond overgeneralization that assumes that human development everywhere functions in the same ways as in researchers' own communities, and to be able to account for both similarities and differences across communities." (Barbara Rogoff, 2003)

Moreover, "Understanding development from (*Sociocultural-historical or Cultural-Historical*) perspective requires examination of the cultural nature of everyday life. This includes studying people's use and transformation of cultural tools and technologies and their involvement in cultural traditions in the structures and institutions of family life and community practices." (Rogoff & Chavajay, 1995).

If society can move beyond the stigma that one way is better than another then the possibilities to consider another cultural perspective and trying to understand how their system works and respecting their time and place, then cultural traditions will remain, yet psychologist will have an understanding on the cultural perspective to respect its nature. "Many communities cultural practice is objectionable. Cultural practices fit together and are connected. Each needs to understand the relation to other aspects of the cultural approach. Cultural process involved multifaceted relations among many aspects of community functioning; they are not just a collection of variables to operate independently. Rather they vary together in patterned ways." (Barbara Rogoff, 2003).

References

1. Biehl. M. Mastumoto, D., Ekman, P., Hearn, V. Heider, K., Kerdoh, T., & Ton., V. (1997).Mastsumoto and Ekman's Japanese and Caucasian Facial Expression of Emotion (JACFEE) Reliability data and cross-national differences. Journal of nonverbal behavior, (210), pg.3-22.
2. Carl Ratner (2003). Journal of Theory of Social Behavior: Theoretical and Methodological problem in Cross Cultural Psychology, 33. P. 67-94.
3. Carl Ratner (1999). Cultural Psychology: A Critique Cultural Dynamics 11, p.7-31. Website:http://www.sonicnet/`cr2/L
4. Carl Ratner (2006). Cultural psychology: A Perspective on Psychological Functioning and Social reform.
5. Christine Welzel, Ronald Inglehart & Hans Dieter Klingemann, (2003). European Consortium for Political Research, 42: pg. 341-379.
6. David Mastsumoto, (1989). Cultural Differences on the Perception of Emotion. Journal of Cross-Cultural Psychology, 20(1), pg.92-105.
7. David Mastumoto. Cross Cultural psychology in the 21ˢᵗ Century (Chpt 5). Website:http://www.teachpsych.org/ebooks/faces/script/cho5.htm.
8. Hui, C.H., (1988). Measurement of Individualism-Collectivism. Journal of Research in Personality, 22, pg. 17-36.
9. Hunington, S. P. (1996). The clash of Civilization and the remarking of the World Order: New York: Simon & Schuster.
10. IBID: Carl Ratner., Institute for Cultural Research & Education, Child Psychology: Vygotsky's Conception of Psychological Development. Introduction to Section 5.
11. Peng & Nisbet, (1999). Culture, dialectics and reasoning about contradiction. American Psychologist, 54(9), pg. 741-754; Peng, Ames, & Knowleses, (2001) Culture and Human Inference: Persepective from three traditions. In D. Masumoto (Ed.), The

Handbook of Culture and Psychology.; Ji, Peng, & Nisbett, (2000). The Culture of Control, and Perception of relationship in the environment. Journal of Personality and Social Psychology, 78(5), pg.943-945.; Nisbett, Ping, Choi, & Norenzayan A. (2001). Culture and Systems of thought: Holistic Versus Analytic Cognition Psychology Review. 108(2), pg291-310.

12. Rogoff, Barbara (2003). Paradise. R., Melfa Arauz, R. Correar Cahvez, M., & Angelillo. C. (2003). First learning through intent participation annual review of psychology, 54.

13. Rogoff, Barabara & Chavajay, (1995). Whats become of research on the Cultural basis of Cognitive Development? American Psychologist, 50, 889-977.

14. Triandis, H.C., Leung, K., Villareal, M., & Clack, F.L., (1985). Allocentric Verse Idocentric tendencies: Convergent and Discrimination Validation. Journal of research and personality, 19, pg. 395-415.

15. Singlelis, T.H., Triandis, H.C., Bhawuk, D.P.S., and Gelfand, M.J. (1995). Horizontal and Vertical aspects of individualism and Collectivism: A Theoretical and Measurement refinement, Cross-Cultural Research, 29, pg.240-275.

16. Yamaguchi, L.A., & Tharp, R.G., (1994). Policy and the Development of effective Education for Native Americans. Paper presented at the meeting of the American Educational Research Associates: New Orleans.

Of the following ten approaches, select at least three and discuss how you would utilize these particular approaches in the diagnosis and treatment of major depression. For each, describe a case in which the approach you select would be the treatment of choice when compared to others. Discuss why you believe that these three approaches are more effective than the remaining seven in the treatment of major depression. Include a consideration of the role of medication or other medical interventions (i.e., when, why, and how should it be implemented? Etc.,)

Psychoanalytic therapy	Gestalt therapy	Reality therapy
Adlerian therapy	Behavior Therapy	Feminist therapy
Existential therapy	Cognitive Behavior therapy	Family systems therapy
Person-centered therapy		

Psychotherapy

Psychotherapy

In general describes many psychological disorders and mental problems, the main focus is to hone in on a specific mental illness or a life stressor, and this depends on how the clinical psychologist want to approach the mental health concern. Psychotherapy is seen as a *"Distinctive"* mental health profession, however many psychologist partake in this psychological career field. Psychotherapy is used in many different ways and approaches depending on the therapist.

According to the national Institute of Mental Health (NIMA), "Psychotherapy is a way to treat clients with mental disorders by helping them understand their illness. Psychotherapy teaches clients strategies and gives them the tools to deal with stress and unhealthy thoughts. Psychotherapy aides in the management of clients being to keep handle on their lives and being able to live more healthy life.

Further according NIMH, "There are many kinds of Psychotherapy; there is no "One- size-fits- all" approach some clients may have a treatment plan that involves only one type of psychotherapy. Others receive treatment that includes elements of several difficult types. The kind of psychotherapy a person received depends on their needs.

Some of the ***best treatment approaches*** that are used in **psychotherapy** that I will discuss in this written exam are:

A. **Cognitive Behavioral Therapy**
B. **Psychoanalytic Therapy**
C. **Behavior Therapy**

Cognitive Behavioral Therapy (CBT)

Is a highly recognized form of treatment of mental illness and is recognized by the American Board of Professional Psychology, many educational programs have incorporated CBT in their instruction curriculums, and also in the professional world of mental health treatment professions. CBT in general terms is the process in changing thought patterns and irrational thinking and is effective in treating depression and anxiety.

Psychologist work to changed behaviors through years of reinforcement, for example I myself have phobias such as fear of heights, elevators, spiders the goal for myself is to face my fears (called desensitization), in dealing with my phobias, with repetitive reinforcement of the process of dealing with my fears head on, it will help the fear to diminish over time. In my circle of family, depression, and severe mental illness is the family genetic trait. Clinical depression is the overall culprit of mental illness within my family. In this written exam I will address the family members suffering from major depression based on years of observation and experience in dealing with immediate family members dealing with depression, and other major depressive disorders.

In a case of a family member who married at the young age of fifteen, and didn't realize she married a drug abuser who was abusive, who later sold all their worldly belonging for crack cocaine, it took this family member into tail spin of depression, she begin to isolate herself from family members, and would never come out of the house, she stayed in the dark all the time, always asleep, didn't eat very much, shared no laughter of smiles, always looking sad as if it was dooms day, and one day she called me to tell me she loved me and that she was proud of me. I really didn't know what to think at the time. However I, thought it was odd and later that night I went skating, only to get a phone call at the skating rink that my family member had tried to commit suicide by a combination of alcohol and pill overdose.

During this time I was working on my bachelor's degree in psychology. For this family member the depression went untreated until it was almost too late, the family member barely survived the overdose. "Depression is a medical illness that causes a persistent feeling of sadness and loss of interest along with a host of other psychological symptoms. Depression can also cause physical symptoms too. For some people depression symptoms are so severe that it's debilitating and a clear tail-tail sign for others they may feel miserable and unhappy without knowing why or realizing they may be experiencing some form of depression." (Mayo Clinic). Depression can be mild to moderate in nature.

The treatment choice

For this family member it would be a complete assessment of the client and her family history of mental illness and history of the client's life, a psychological test would be conducted such as SASSI or MAYSI to identify any substance abuse usage related to the psychological symptoms to determine whether dual diagnosis is present in addition to any pre-existing mental disorders. Based on the outcomes of the assessment and only identifying severe depression with suicidal thoughts, and injury to self, the client would be admitted for inpatient treatment services and placed under 24hr suicide watch protection until the symptoms decrease based on clinical assessment tool rating criteria scores are below minimal risk.

The focus would be intensive cognitive behavioral therapy to deal with severe depression and the focus it to desensitize the dysfunctional way of thinking that makes a person become depressed. According to Beck et al., (1979), "Specific interventions are suggested for each part of the triad, as well as for alleviating the bodily behavioral, and emotional symptoms of depression that are triggered by this way of thinking."

Therefore, it would be necessary to formulate an effective treatment plan and techniques for assessing the progression of therapeutic services to elevate or diminished the clinical depression. According to Klerman, Weissman, Rounsaville, and Clevron (1984)." The group of scholars has created a manual of short-term therapy of depression that is based on interpersonal principles and process, their conceptualization of depression of which the patient is currently engaged.

Dysfunctional thinking affect mood and behavior are assumed to be consequences of these interactional deficits or conflicts. "Four problem areas are considered to be contributory to the onset and maintenance of depression to one degree or another; (1) grief and bereavement, (2) interpersonal conflict with significant others in patients immediate life; (3) role transitions and changes in areas such as employment; residence economic status, marriage and parenting; and gaps in interpersonal skills that inhibit successful engagement with others and so leads to isolation and loneliness.

Therefore cognitive therapy with a combination of drug therapy was efficacious in reducing vegetative symptoms of depression, including sleep disturbance loss of appetite and somatic distress." (Salvatore Cullari 1998).

Why is the approach more effective?

The practice of cognitive behavioral therapy has been a long standing form of psychotherapy since over 100 years, and is universally used throughout the world in mental health care. "Advances in cognitive-behavioral therapy; Cognitive behavioral therapist have begun to focus their attention on personality disorders." (Beck, Freeman & Associates, 1989). And, "On development process and structure of personality and on schemas and unconscious cognitive processing." (Guidana, 1987).

Behavioral cognitive therapy is moving into an evolutionary era of learning to identify even more so with self and the environmental surroundings as the world evolves. Most drug treatment facilities, and clinicians primarily focus on cognitive behavioral therapy (CBT). Cognitive behavioral therapy can be applied to many specific mental disorders. "Many studies have shown that (CBT) is a particularly effective treatment for depression, especially minor or moderate depression. Some people with depression may be successfully treated with CBT only, however in the case of the family member both therapy and medication was necessary since the family member had suffered from long term clinical depression.

Many clients may need both CBT and medication since it helps with depression and restructuring negative thoughts patterns. Doing so helps clients interpret their environment and interactions with others in a positive and realistic way. "It may also help a person recognize things that may be contributing to depression and help him or her change behaviors that may be making the depression worse." (NIMH, Psychotherapies).

Role of medications or interventions

There are a large number of depression drug treatment medications available and very effective for the most part. Only licensed M.D, treat mental health clients in most cases of moderate to severe depression. Sometime a client may need a combination of medications for the treatment of depression. The types of anti-depressant medications used for the treatment of depression are selective serotonin reuptake inhibitors (SSRIs) listed in the following modalities:

1. Celexa
2. Paxil
3. Prozac
4. Zoloft
5. Lexapro

These are most of the popular antidepressants prescribed to clients suffering from depression and in the case of the family member a combination of medications was prescribed. Other medications used to help with depression are Serotonin and Norepinephrine (SNRIs):

1. Effexor
2. Pristiq
3. Cymbalta

Most A-typical antidepressants are used with a combination of medications for instance to name a few are the Norepinephrine and Dopamine Reuptake Inhibitors called:

1. Wellbutrin
2. Rameron
3. Oleptro

These medications are generally prescribed in combination with others to aid sleep. With all the medication readily available to clients based on need and a full assessment of the clients psychological problem determines the mediation to be prescribed to ensure the client is getting the essential medication needed to treat their current mental health condition.

According to many mental health care scholars mental health medications takes up to two weeks to feel the full effect of the medications to start working. before they begin to fully work appropriately. Although a variable of medications may be necessary to stabilize a client it is essential in order for the client to be a productive member of society. ***Preventive medicine,*** there are a variance of alternative medicine strategies that a client can engage themselves in for instance; meditation classes, yoga, group therapy sessions, stress classes, anxiety classes, coping classes. Alternative medicine such as St. Johns Worth, Ginseng, Gingko, along with herbal teas said to ease the mind, and help with suppressing mental illness symptoms of depression.

Finally, According to Pomerantz, (2008) he states, "There are widely recognized pioneers of cognitive therapy: Albert Ellis and Aaron Beck cognitive therapist strive to achieve a positive therapy outcome quite quickly- typically in less than 15 sessions, but significantly longer in complex or severe cases (J.S. Beck, 1996 2002; Roth et al., 2002).

Psychoanalytic Therapy,

According to Cherry, (2013),"Psychoanalytic therapy is one of the most well-known treatment modalities, yet is one of the most understandable by mental health consumers. This type of therapy is based upon the theories and work of Sigmund Freud. Who founded the school of psychology known as Psychoanalysis."

Psychoanalytic therapy focuses on the unconscious mind and the impact it has on client's behaviors and thoughts. Therapist conducts assessments going back to early childhood to determine if past experiences involve current issues today. Clients who have therapy may seek it for months or years depending on each person's label of therapy needed to control thoughts and behaviors.

Case

Some clients experience a serve case of insomnia and anxiousness during exams, waiting for test results, and scheduling events; or expecting longtime friends and since anxiety is a state of anticipation both insomnia and anxiety can go hand-in-hand. Resulting in an extreme emotion the clients are expecting to move in or anticipate outcomes from the intense anxiety and lack of sleep is driven by the anticipation of various outcomes, expected events from the clients results in the client's inability to allow their mind to rest, due to racing emotions.

According to, Carl. E. Pletsch (2008), "Psychoanalysts are of course not all fully aware of the fact that case studies play such an important role in their discipline. Many if not most psychoanalysts are still consciously wedded to a positivistic conception of science, and they place great store in the theory of psychoanalysis when they represent it to the public at large.

Whatever one thinks of psychoanalysis, it is a fact that Freud's case studies have been extremely important vehicles of the tradition of psychoanalytic knowledge. The impression is that psychoanalytic case studies Freud's in particular serve the purpose of helping psychoanalysts

Identify the problems posed by their patients and permit psychoanalysts all over the world, sitting done in their consultation rooms with their patients, to proceed in parallel fashion, *even though the examples are not always successful."*

Sigmund Freud (left) with his friend Wilhelm Fleiss. Beside Freud, Fleiss played an important role in the birth of psychoanalysis.

Treatment Choice

Therapist generally gathers information on the client that is specific to the problem the client is dealing with to help the client deal with their problem or identify the cause. Therapist generally can solve problems in one or three sessions to dealing with client's problems for many years depending on the seriousness of each client's problems.

"The approach to treatment is considered successful if the patient has shown:

- Reduction in intensity of number of symptoms
- Some resolution of basic emotional thoughts
- Increase independence and self-esteem
- Improved functioning and adaptation to life

"Attempts to compare the effectiveness of psychoanalytic treatment of other modes of therapy are difficult to evaluate. Some aspects of Freudian theory have been questioned since the 1970s on the grounds of their psychoanalysis presupposes a highly individualistic Western concept of human personhood that is alien to traditional Asian and African societies. Moreover, this is general agreement to psychoanalytic approaches worldwide for certain type of patients, specifically those with neurotic conflicts." (Medical Mosby's Dictionary).

Role of medication or intervention

Medications that are generally used in psychotherapies are also used in the previous psychotherapies discussed according to each patients need. Further, if a client enters into "long-term "Intensive psychoanalytic treatment with a well-qualified clinician, the client will have a very good chance of achieving the goals of relieving the problems that may have caused the client to seek treatment in the first place. It will take time and commitment on the client's part as well as the therapist." (Canadian Psychoanalytic Society).

Behavioral Therapy

Behaviorism is the concept adapted in the terms of behavioral therapy, a behavior that many of use learn from within our homes or environment, or social settings. The overarching goal of behavioral therapy is to reinforce behaviors and eradicate undesirable behaviors or maladaptive behaviors.

The modalities used in this process are generally classical conditioning and operant conditioning. For the most respect behavioral therapy is action based. Psychologist focused on the same patterns of behaviors that lead up to the behavioral problem. Therefore behavioral therapy is focused based, and the goal is to show client's ways to change their behavior in order to minimize their current behavioral problems and learns new positive behaviors.

According to Whinston, (2000), "Negative reinforcement is another contingency whereby a child learns through consequences of his or her behavior. "With positive reinforcement the outcomes of negative reinforcement is increasingly (a reinforcing) the future of probability behavior. In negative reinforcement where stimulus is applied after the occurrence of a behavior, the removal of this stimulus is associated with an increase in the original behavior." Moreover, in escape earning the youngster is exposed to a stimulus that the child experiences as aversive, this child learns to avoid that stimulus through an increase in some behavior. For example, if a child who is sensitive to criticism is criticized for not cleaning his room, he will likely increase his room cleaning behavior in order to avoid receiving criticism. Behavioral therapy is also associated with children who have attention deficit disorders. Behavioral therapy is more widely used in children than adults.

Treatment Choice

The medication best used for behavioral or emotional problems faced by clients or youths are stimulants such as methylphenidate or dextroamphetamine. These medications are generally used by children suffering from attention deficit disorder. Although there are other medications associated with behavioral problems and many of them are have been mention previously under the listed psychotherapies in alignment with the client's mental health issues common usage are antidepressants and bupropion to mention a few.

What approach is more effective?

"Behavioral management principles include techniques for giving instruction's and commands in a way that builds a client's self-esteem. Programs that teach behavior therapy focus on how to give clear commands use of time out effectively create effective rewards system, in otherwise structure an environment that will work." (American Academy of Pediatrics, 2011). When it comes to behavior therapy several modalities may have to be approached as a means to best identify what works best for the client and the treatment approach.

According to Wikipedia, "Behavior therapy does not involve one specific method but it has a wide range of techniques that can be used to treat a person's psychological problems. Behavior therapy that can be broken down into three disciplines:

(1). Applied Behavioral Analysis

(2). Cognitive Behavior Therapy

(3). Habit Reversal Training

Applied behavioral analysis, focus on operant conditioning in form of positive reinforcement to modify behavior after conducting a functional Behavior Assessment."

Role of medication or intervention

The role of behavioral therapy approach can be more effective in treating clients with behavioral problems. The medication is used as a method of controlling the behavior of the client to focus more effectively, and respond better to the commands of behavior management techniques. Other interventions as previously stated is working toward self-esteem, and building a client's self-worth, along with building up the client's confidence using techniques such as long tern behavioral intervention workshops, and individual sessions.

The three approaches, verse the other psychotherapies

Cognitive Behavioral Therapy, Psychoanalytic Therapy, & Behavior Therapy, in reference to, Adlerian Therapy, Existential therapy, Person-Centered-therapy, Gestalt therapy, Reality Therapy, Feminist Therapy, Family Systems Therapy, are all unique in their own skill set psychotherapy specialty. Universally all of the psychotherapy services are rendered to a vast majority of the population needing specific therapy sessions. However, globally and universally the practice of choice for many clinician have been "Cognitive Behavioral Therapy" and "Behavior Therapy" for most of the younger population & Psychoanalytic therapy rising to the occasion in the new era of further development, with the other psychotherapies following in growth and expanding to meet the needs of many cultures globally.

References

1. American Academy of pediatrics, (2011). What every parent needs to know Website:http://www.healthychildren.org

2. Beck, A.T., Rush, A.J., Shaw, J., & Emory. G (1979). Cognitive Therapy of Depression. New York: Guild Press.

3. Beck, A.T., Freeman, A, & Associates, (1989). Cognitive Therapy of Personality Disorders. New York: Guild Press.

4. Canadian Psychoanalytic Society: What is the outcome of Psychoanalytic Treatment? Website:http//www.en.psychoanalysis.ca/aboutpsychoanalysis/what-is-the-outcome-of-psychoanalytic-treatment.

5. Carl. E. Pletsch, (2008). Freud's Case Studies and the Locus of Psychoanalytic Knowledge (p.265).

6. Freud.(Picture). What is Psychology Website: freudfile.org/psychoanalysis/definition.html

7. Guidano, V. F. (1987). Complexity of the Self. New York: Guildford Press.

8. Kendra Cherry, (2012). What is Psychoanalytic Therapy? About.comGuide. Website:http://www.psychology.about-com/od/pindex/psychoanalytic.therapy.htm

9. Home Health & Education Mental Health Information, NINH –Psychotherapies Website. http://www.nimh.nih.gov/health/topics/psychotherapies

10. Klerman, G.L., Weissman, M.M., Rounsaville, B.J., & Cheveron, E.S. (1984). Inter-personal Psychotherapy of Depression. New York: Basic Books.

11. Mayo Clinic Staff, (2012). Depression (Major Depression) Website. http://www.mayoclinic.com

12. Mosby's Medical Dictionary, (2009),. 8th Edition Website:http://www.medical-dictionary.thefreedictionary.com/psycholytic+treatment

13. Salvatori Cullari, (1998). Foundation of Clinical Psychology

14. National Institute of health (NIMH). Psychotherapies: Home health & Education Mental health Information. Website:http://www.nimh.nih.gov/health/psychotherapies/index.sh.html
15. Wikipedia. Behavior Therapy Website:http://www.en.wikipedia.org/wiki/bahviortherapy.

escribe the evolution of the field of health psychology. Discuss the biopsychosocial model, its application, and its influence on current research in the area of health psychology. What do you see as the strengths and weakness of this model? What emerging trends do you see that will impact the field of health psychology and how do you expect that it will change?

Knowledge: Health Psychology

As time and evolution evolves there will be many challenges that psychologist will face in regards to the understanding of health and psychology. Health psychology strives to understand the many medical diseases American's face today and the dynamics of psychology as it relates to our health.

According to MacDonald (2013), "The world of health psychology is changing lives one day at a time and with some expert guidance and support people experience the healthy, vibrant life that they desire and all it takes is unlocking the secrets of the brain, body, and emotions. A simple fact of life is that human beings are extraordinary complex, and an illness can be the result of myriad of factors. These factors emerged from biological, psychological, and environmental facets of everyday life. Often medications alone will not provide the positive results necessary for people to achieve maximum health."

Further, as we move into a new era of evolution the practice of health psychology will be more prevalent and the practice will improve the likelihood of individuals stopping their addiction. Over time health psychology will aid in the following, individuals working on their health and becoming more physically fit, and health psychologist helping in the reduction of chronic pain, and improving the quality of life in helping individuals better cope with their health problems, and establishing coping mechanism and dealing with stressors. The overall goal is to help individuals cope with everyday life and achieve their goals by providing techniques that will help individuals to manage their medical condition.

According to Matarazzo (1980), "Health psychology can be understood in terms of the same questions that were asked of the biomedical model:

What causes illness? Health psychology suggests that human beings should be seen as complex systems and that illness is caused by a multitude of factors and not by a single causal factor. Health psychology therefore attempts to move away from a simple linear model of health and claims that illness can be caused by a combination of biological (e.g. a virus), psychological (e.g. behaviors, beliefs) and social (e.g. employment) factors. This approach reflects the *bio psychosocial model of health and illness*, which was developed by Engel (1977, 1980) and is illustrated in Figure 1.1.

The bio psychosocial model represented an attempt to integrate the psychological (the 'Psycho') and the environmental (the 'social') into the traditional biomedical (the 'bio') model of health as follows: (1) The *bio* contributing factors included genetics, viruses, bacteria and structural defects. (2) The *psycho* aspects of health and illness were described in terms of cognitions (e.g. expectations of health), emotions (e.g. fear of treatment), and behaviors (e.g. smoking, diet, exercise or alcohol consumption)."

Bio:	Psycho:	Social:
• Viruses	• Behavior	• Class
• Bacteria's	• Beliefs	• Employment
• Lesions	• Coping	• Ethnicity
	• Stress	
	• Pain	

Fig. 1-1 The Bio-psycho-social model of health and illness (after Engel 1997-1980)

"The origins of health and psychology rest in a combination of biology, medicine, physiology, philosophy, and social science. Health psychology interfaces with the field of epidemiology and public health and contributes to improvement in health by increasing knowledge about how health can best be achieved. The work of clinical health psychologist sometimes intersects with the fields of nursing, social work, excise science, and other disciplines aimed toward understanding and changing health-related behavior. Health and psychology is a science as well as profession. (Papas, Belar, & Rozensky, 2004).

Moreover, according to Matarazzo (1980), "Health psychology regards psychological factors not only as possible consequences of illness but as contributing to its etiology. Health Psychologists considers both a direct and indirect association between psychology and health. The direct pathway is reflected in the physiological literature and is illustrated by research exploring the impact of stress on illnesses such as coronary heart disease and cancer.

Our health, have a grave impact on our ability to control our mind thoughts and how many of us get through the healing process by keeping a sound mind with positive thoughts. This thought provoking attitude helps the body to heal faster. Worry takes a toll on the body's ability to fight the immune system. Sometimes our mind can destroy our ability to heal based on constantly worrying about your illness.

From this perspective the way a person experience's their life ('I am feeling stressed') has a direct impact upon their body which can change their health status. The indirect pathway is reflected more in the behavioral literature and is illustrated by research exploring smoking, diet, exercise and sexual behavior. From this perspective, the ways a person thinks ('I am feeling stressed') influences their behavior ('I will have a cigarette') which in turn can impact upon their health. "

According to Suls & Rothman, (2004) "The idea that the mind and the body together determine health and illness logically implies a model for studying these issues. This model is called the **bio psychosocial model.** As its name implies, its fundamental assumption is that health and illness are consequences of the interplay of biological, psychological, and social factors."

The mind and body relationship brief history

"Historically, philosophers have vacillated between the view that the mind and body are part of the same system and the idea that they are two separate systems. When we look at ancient history, it becomes clear that we have come full circle in our beliefs about the mind-body relationship. During human prehistory, most cultures regarded the mind and body as intertwined.

Disease was thought to arise when evil spirits entered the body, and treatment consisted primarily of attempts to exorcise these spirits. Some skulls from the Stone Age have small, symmetrical holes that are believed to have been made intentionally with sharp tools to allow the evil spirit to leave the body while the shaman performed the treatment ritual." See picture (1), depicting images. (Introduction to Health Psychology Part 1.)

Picture (1) Above

"Sophisticated, though not always successful, techniques for the treatment of illness were developed during the Renaissance. This woodcut from the 1570s depicts a surgeon drilling a hole in a patient's skull, with the patient's family and pets looking on."

The bio psychosocial strength and weakness of health psychology are:

Weaknesses

- Some critics point out this question of distinction and of determination of the roles of illness and disease.
- This may be exploited by medical insurance companies or government welfare departments eager to limit or deny access to medical and social care.
- Epstein and colleagues describe six conflicting interpretations of what the model might be, and proposes that "...habits of mind may be the missing link between a bio psychosocial intent and clinical reality."
- Psychiatrist Hamid Tavakoli argues that the BPS model should be avoided because it unintentionally promotes an artificial distinction between biology and psychology, and merely causes confusion in psychiatric assessments and training programs, and that ultimately it has not helped the cause of trying to de-stigmatize mental health.
- From an epistemological (theory of knowledge) stand there can be no model of mental disorder without first establishing a theory of the mind.
- Problems with testability: difficult to test empirically (with experiments)
- Unclear how exactly the factors interact

Strengths

- A BPS model focuses attention on the diversity of client needs, reinforcing the importance of client-centered clinical practices.
- A BPS model includes traditional addictions models as therapeutic options. It provides a broad and flexible framework for conceptualizing the nature of the problem and for selecting from a wide range of potentially effective responses to it.

- The BPS model is amenable to empirical scrutiny and supports a broad range of empirically tested "best practices".
- Commonsensical, palpable. Has provided a framework for treatment and future research.

Less reductionist emphasize an interaction of several factors

Emerging trends and impact in field of health psychology and expected change

Are inevitable from historical times to today's evolution of time and change health and psychology is moving in a more innovative direction were the field of psychology is more connected to understanding the psychological impact and influences on individuals to stay more physically fit and healthy through health and promotion, through the news media, and internet blogs, and social media networks.

Health psychology in today's trends further focuses more on maintaining preventative measures in health and illness and dysfunction. The overall arching goals as we move forward with innovative trends in health and psychology are to establish a large geographical network of community health and wellness promotion through our communication networking systems of mental health care and delivery systems. "According to health and psychology chapter (1), "The bio psychosocial models guides health psychologist in their efforts to uncover factors that predicts states of health and illness and in their clinical interventions with patients."

References

1. Dr. Cheryl MacDonald, R.N. PsyD. (2013). Health Psychology Center Presents: What is Health Psychology. Website: healthpsychology.org/what-is-health-psychology.
2. Engel, G.L. (1977). The need for a new medical model: A challenge for Bio-Medicine. Science, 196, 129-136.
3. Introduction to Health Psychology Chapter 1. Jones and Barlett Publishers LLC. Website: www.jblearning.com/samples/0763743828/43828_ch01_5183.pdf
4. Matarazzo, J.D. (1980). Behavioral Health and Behavioral Medicine: Frontiers for a new Health Psychology. The American Psychologist. 35 (9) 807-817.
5. Papas, R.K., Belar, C.D. & Rozensky, R.H. (2004). The Practice of Clinical Health Psychology. Professional issue. In R.G. Frank, A. Baum, & J. L. Wallanfer (Eds). Handbook of Clinical Health Psychology, Volume 2 (pp. 293-319). Washington DC: American Psychological Association.
6. Suls, J. 7 Rothman A, (2004). Evolution of the biopsychosocial model: prospects and challenges for health psychology. Website: htttp://www.ncbi.nlm.nih.gov/pubmed

Conclusions

Professional Ethics

"The Ethics Code is intended to provide guidance for psychologist and standards of professional conduct that can be applied by the APA and by other bodies that choose to adopt them." (American Psychological Association).

These Codes provide the parameters within which professional judgments should be made. However, it cannot, and does not aim to, provide the answer to every ethical dilemma a

Psychologist may face. It is important to remember to reflect and apply a process to resolve ethical dilemmas as set out in this code. (The British psychological Society, 2009). The five principles principle are the founding authorities to providing optimum care to clients in need of services deliverable is the best humanly possible way to deliver.

Assessments

In this era assessment testing is continuingly being tested and challenged. Psychologist must profess their level of expertise and competence to be able to perform such testing. Conducting assessment on clients may have a dramatic impact on them based on the results given, therefore it is essential that psychologist make certain that the client is apprised of the results in a according to Whinston, (2000), "Professional and ethical manner." Assessments are always the "bench mark" in beginning the process of identifying any aspect of problems associated to humans. It sets the precedence for identifying and diagnosing many facets of behaviors associated with humans.

Developmental Psychology

Developmental psychology serves its purpose the field of understanding scientific changes that occur in "Human beings over the course of their life span" (Wikipedia). Developmental psychology focuses on the behavior of c individuals and environmental factors, and cultural perspectives, social context, and the impact it has on development.

Psychotherapy

According to Mayo Clinic, (2013), "There are many specific types of psychotherapy, each with its own approach. The type of psychotherapy that's right for you depends on your individual situation. Psychotherapy is also known as talk therapy, counseling, psychosocial therapy or, simply, therapy. Psychotherapy in moving into the 21st century is becoming more innovative and more community based to reach a much broader population through devices such as networks, communication technology.

Health and Psychology

"The Biopsychosocial model guides health psychologist in their research efforts to uncover factors that predict states of health and illness and in their clinical intervention with patients." (What is Health Psychology Chapter 1). Health and Psychology goes "*hand and hand*" there are many aspects of psychology that takes impacts the mental state of minds of humans, and the overarching goal is to be able to control our thought process, as it may have impact on many of us health wise.

References

1. American Psychological Association (2010). Ethical Principles of Psychologist and Code of Conduct.
2. Introduction to Health Psychology Part (1). Website: http://ww.highered.mcgrawhill.com/taylor7e.chpt1.pdf.
3. Mayo Clinic, (2013). Psychotherapy. Mayo Clinic Staff. Website:http://www.mayoclinic.com/health/psychotherapy/MY00186
4. Wikipedia Website: Wikipedia.com